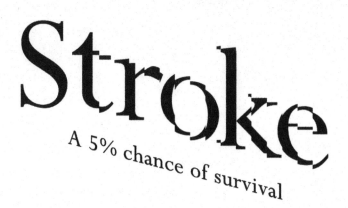

Stroke

A 5% chance of survival

Ricky Monahan Brown

SANDSTONE PRESS

First published in Great Britain by
Sandstone Press Ltd
Dochcarty Road
Dingwall
Ross-shire
IV15 9UG
Scotland

www.sandstonepress.com

Translation of Hon'ami Kōetsu poem reproduced by kind
permission of the Philadelphia Museum of Art

The publisher acknowledges subsidy from Creative
Scotland towards publication of this volume.

ISBN: 978-1-912240-44-9
ISBNe: 978-1-912240-45-6

Cover design by Mark Swan
Typeset by Biblichor Ltd, Edinburgh
Printed and bound by Totem, Poland

For you, Pickle. Obvs.

Author's Note

As I write in these pages, many survivors of strokes, brain haemorrhages and brain injuries have stories about their experiences that have been practiced many times. We find our way to narratives that make some sort of sense of those experiences and our losses. I've tried my best to tell my story accurately in a way that makes sense to me. Some names and identifying characteristics have been changed to preserve anonymity, and a composite character or two appears herein. Throughout most of this story, my brain is broken, and I hope you'll make allowances for that.

1

You Had an Orgasm, I Had a Stroke

Like all the best boy meets girl, they fall in love, boy suffers catastrophic brain injury stories, this one started on a normal day. My girlfriend Beth and I had arranged to take my ten-year-old daughter on a playdate with a schoolmate to the New York Hall of Science. Six hundred eccentrics were displaying their glorified high school science projects as part of the World Maker Faire, among them an amateur mad scientist who was presenting his *Zombie Detector Machine*.

The detector worked simply enough. Professor Frankenstein read a set of simple questions from his script. 'Have you travelled abroad in the past year?'

'Yes. We visited my father in Edinburgh in February.'

He tapped away at the machine. 'Have you recently suffered any bites?'

We were in New York, and it was September. 'I'm almost certainly being bitten by a mosquito right now!'

Tap-tap-tap.

'And do you ever experience a craving for brains?

Since I seemed to be in enough trouble already, I figured that I might as well admit to a regular craving for haggis from a butcher just across the Hudson River in New Jersey, and all the warm-reeking, gushing entrails that might involve. Besides, Beth and I were vegetarians, so the haggis we would actually order was meat-free and my admission of having eaten haggis around the anniversary of the Declaration of Arbroath (or, as we would have it in New York, *Tartan Day*) was no worse than an admission that I might have been eating kidney bean brains. Even if that would be two sets of organs for the price of one.

Frankenstein handed me a lightweight metal box and instructed me to press a button. When the button was pressed, the front of the box would light up to spell out either the word *HUMAN* or the word *ZOMBIE*, and the participant, applicably labelled, would show up on the monitor included in the exhibit.

My answers added up to only one conclusion. The blood was daubed on the wall – I was a *ZOMBIE*.

Beth was *HUMAN*, but my daughter Elizabeth was a *ZOMBIE*, too, so I wasn't too concerned about my diagnosis. In fact, being a practically invincible member of the undead army could have been seen as a boon. For a start, there were more life and death scenarios to be navigated at the Faire.

Elizabeth and I climbed into a submarine simulator, within which a pair of participants had to complete a set of instructions and tasks – press this button, spin that wheel – to avoid having a load of water dumped on them. Not exactly the *Lusitania*, I thought to myself, but it was certainly a bit soggy. In the end, even that was neither here nor there, as a rainstorm opened up over Queens and we were all soaked to the skin soon enough.

That was the last time I felt rain on my cheek the way a person is supposed to.

The Hall of Science and its grounds began to empty, and the three of us got the subway back to Brooklyn. We dropped Elizabeth off with her mother, a drive-by drop off, since my estranged wife and I had been separated for over two years. Our divorce had been sliding towards the acrimonious, and most of our conversations would end with her calling me an asshole.

We left all that behind, returned home to pick up our pink Malaguti scooter, and rode out to Red Hook for a game of pool in a quiet little bar. We hit the back room and had a couple of beers while sinking a few balls. Although I had recently been labelled as one of the undead, my hand-eye coordination held up pretty well, and we halved four games. We whiled away some more of the early evening chatting with the motorcycle-loving proprietors, and by the time we were pulling our helmets on to head back to South Park Slope, Beth and I were convinced we were the coolest, most charming couple in the borough, what with our sexy moped, our pool skills, our bar-owning, hog-riding friends, and a skinful of beer. We luxuriated in each other's company a little longer, and headed to Toby's to share some pizza and a couple of large glasses of Italian red. An excellent meal, in lovely company, that fully deserved to be rounded off by a quick smoke, so, as was our wont, we idly chatted over a couple of Parliaments in the late summer air before heading home.

It could hardly have been a more pleasant day. I was able to forget for a moment that the previous day I had been sacked from my job as a financial lawyer in Midtown Manhattan; that other than to visit my mother in hospital and return for her funeral, I hadn't been back home to Scotland for years; that my ex-wife Linda was probably right – I *was* a bit of an asshole. It was good to live in the moment for a moment.

Back at the flat, as I had sex for what would soon seem to be the last time, I couldn't have been more in the moment. For her birthday, I had made Beth a piece of art that listed 32 general things I liked about dating her on one side. On the other side, it listed 32 things I liked about our lovemaking. The feel of her skin was thing 12 on one side, and things 5 and 28 on the other.

Tonight, it felt like a million butterfly wings caressing my flesh.

It wasn't unusual for me to be short of breath after a session. Or to be so awash with dopamine, norepinephrine, oxytocin and other naturally occurring uppers and downers that I would feel nauseous. An inability to string together an articulate thought in the aftermath of our lovemaking was nothing odd. In short, for me to be so intensely affected by our sex that I would complain of feeling 'weird' on this particular day would not be strange.

'Honey, I've got a weird feeling in my left-hand side.'

'What does it feel like? Do you think you're having a heart attack?'

'I don't know,' I replied, thinking of my father's coronaries. 'I mean, I'm not experiencing a vice-like pain in my chest or anything like that.'

'OK. Relax for a minute. Do you need your asthma inhaler?'

'No, I think I just need to lie quietly for a bit. I'll be fine.'

'Good.' She smiled. 'Look, I'm going to kill you with sex one day, but not today.'

It was a fair remark. I was being entirely coherent and calm. We had been having a lovely day. There was no reason to panic. Still, after a minute or two, my left side was still feeling . . . I couldn't describe it. Odd. Tingly. Nervy?

'Sweetie, it might not be such a bad idea to call an ambulance,' I admitted. 'I think I'm going to be OK, but I don't want us to be up all night worrying.'

I had begun to harbour suspicions that I was dying. I remember, very strongly, not wanting to make too much of a big deal about it. We had had a lovely day, and there was no need to spoil it by overreacting to something that, at first, seemed like it might pass with a quick lie down and a glass of water.

'Don't worry.' I smiled. 'Everything's going to be fine.'

That was the last thing I said before I lost consciousness. It wasn't entirely a lie. Beth was bright and smart and funny. I thought she'd do just fine without me.

I was acting like William Bennett, the San Francisco Symphony's principal oboist who suffered a cerebral haemorrhage midway through a performance of Richard Strauss's Oboe Concerto. Bennett managed to fall – or more accurately, collapse – in such a way that, as he went down, he was able to hold his oboe aloft for a violinist to take it from him.

I get it. He didn't want to cause a scene.

Fortunately, Beth had been around enough Scots, and dated this one for long enough, to be able to translate my subtle suggestion that we call an ambulance as *HOLY CRAP! I think I'm dying!*

Curiously, I have no recollection of panic or fear. Before all this happened, I had always been scared of death, but in the face of my own mortality, I was calmly monitoring the way I felt and trying to communicate with my girlfriend about how things were progressing. As well as having the sexual charge to kill a man, Beth is scary smart and very practical. If I ever needed a layperson to give me sound advice about how to proceed as the feeling was receding in my left side and my brain was literally exploding, she'd be the person I'd choose. What I thought swiftly became irrelevant as I lost consciousness, becoming blind and deaf to the mess, puke and snot that were accompanying my departure from this mortal coil.

As Beth coped with my post-coital passing and the arrival of the emergency medical technicians who staffed the ambulance, I was somewhere altogether more pleasant: standing in my late grandfather Hugh's back garden in Buckie. Not only could I see it perfectly in my mind's eye, I could feel the sandy, coastal Morayshire soil running through my hands. Given what I later found out was going on in my head, the illusion I conjured for myself was miraculous.

Surprisingly, the garden served as a setting for diagnostics, where I could perform some scientific experimentation in a safe environment. Although Beth and I had been worried about the possibility of a heart attack, given my racing heart and the strange sensations on my left-hand side, my unconscious self had other concerns. The clear difference in feeling on my left and right sides had me worrying about a stroke, which only became apparent to me as I wandered through the hallucination of Hugh's back garden. Like the real garden had been twenty years previously, it was sectioned into six squarish areas. Each part corresponded to a different part of my body. Looked at from above, the upper-left part of the garden, closest to the house, represented the left side of my face. It was a bit of a mess, frankly, and overgrown. Not the way I remembered it at all.

As I noticed this, I somehow became aware that I couldn't feel the left side of my face. I resolved to spend the remainder of my time in Buckie figuring out what was going on. I was worried about my face. If I was having a stroke, it was related to hot times with a beautiful woman, and I didn't want that sort of thing being messed up by having a droopy face. Back in the real world I might have been concerned about dying, but here I was going to wander around that bloody garden until I had convinced myself that my face was OK. Even if I couldn't do that, it was peaceful here.

'I could stay here forever,' I thought.

Then, somewhere else in my mind, I saw a sparkle of garnet in Beth's hazel iris, and I knew that I'd crawl over my own corpse to see her one more time.

While I was enjoying a spring afternoon in a mostly well-tended Morayshire garden, Beth had called for that ambulance I'd suggested. This was a good thing. The first important step in surviving and recovering from a stroke is getting prompt medical attention. Apparently, clot-busting medication can reduce the odds of suffering a long-term disability if administered within three hours of the first symptom. Not that clot busting would do me the slightest bit of good: I was having a *haemorrhagic* stroke, not an *ischemic* stroke; my stroke was the result of blood vessels bursting in my brain because of massively elevated blood pressure, not any clotting in those blood vessels.

The reputation that strokes have for being an old person's affliction is understandable. Ischemic strokes account for the vast majority of strokes. The focus on the clot-based nature of most strokes makes them sound sluggish, particularly when combined with the way popular culture tends to depict the stroke victim. Slow-moving. Slurring. A bit like a zombie.

That is to say, strokes are not always dramatic. My fellow survivor of cerebral haemorrhage, the legendary Edinburgh-born musician Edwyn Collins, took a characteristically louche and well-mannered approach to his stroke, even ascribing the feelings of nausea and vertigo he experienced to food poisoning. A full two days passed before he was admitted to intensive care and his major cerebral haemorrhage was diagnosed.

My cerebral haemorrhage, though, was not a cardie-and-slippers event. It wasn't even an indie music, Postcard Records stroke. Fuck, no. It was a punk rock, 1978 Sex Pistols in San Francisco stroke. The lead man in the drama was coughing up blood, the main sentiment being expressed was that this was no fun at all, and nobody could reasonably expect to see the protagonist perform live again.

A haemorrhagic stroke occurs when a blood vessel bursts inside the brain. That doesn't do justice to what had just happened to me as a team of paramedics squeezed into the bedroom. They measured my blood pressure somewhere above 300/200mmHg: high enough to kill two men. A blood vessel 'bursting' inside the brain is, at best, a Green Day stroke. *American Idiot* on Broadway Green Day. Ersatz punk rock. A cerebral haemorrhage at over 300/200mmHg is when a blood vessel *explodes* inside the brain.

We were lucky, then, that we lived just eight short blocks from the nearest hospital. Time is of the essence when responding to a stroke, and it took those paramedics just a few minutes to arrive at our apartment, assess the situation, and remove me to Brooklyn's New York Methodist Hospital.

It's hard for me now to describe the scene at Methodist as I was presented for admission to the emergency room, mainly because I was unconscious. Usually, it's quiet and professional. The large, dark wood admission desk radiates an aura of calm. There are no gurneys slamming through swing doors. I would say that the place has that unmistakable hospital smell, but it doesn't. There's just a pleasant, fresh scent of cleaning supplies. Nothing overpowering.

As one comes through the main hospital entrance into the lobby, a long ramp curves up and to the right, both to cater for the slope that gives the neighbourhood its name, and to allow for the inability of patients, stretchers, IVs and the like to climb stairs. There are skylights everywhere, adding to a pleasant sense of airiness, and giving one a sense of weightlessness.

I've heard stories of other New York emergency rooms where you have to change into a gown in the toilets. 'Not the first one,' the nurse will say. 'It's being cleaned.'

This will be because that first toilet is awash with blood.

Methodist Hospital in Brooklyn, on the other hand, would be as good, as peaceful, a place to die as any.

2

Classy Girl

One of the funny things about a haemorrhagic stroke – and there are a few, I promise – is that the haemorrhagic aspect, the intracerebral bleed, only lasts for maybe ten seconds. About the time it took you to read that sentence. Such a little slice of time for such a devastating event.

While haemorrhagic strokes only account for about fifteen per cent of all strokes, they are responsible for more than thirty per cent of all stroke deaths. My posture as I was rolled into the emergency room indicated that I was comatose and showing signs of severe neurological impairment. That put me at a grade five on the Hunt and Hess scale of diagnosis, with an approximately 90 per cent chance of mortality. If the blunt reality of that wasn't enough, the doctor who turned out to be my neurosurgeon noted that there was a one-in-twenty chance of a 'good outcome', where a good outcome would be surviving in a non-vegetative state, free of serious paralysis.

The paramedics had arrived at our flat within three minutes. Within another five minutes, I was in the emergency room, with more people working on me than Beth could count. The first thing they did was intubate me and hook me up to a ventilator. This is common procedure for the victim of a haemorrhagic stroke, because the patient's impaired consciousness puts them at risk of aspirating saliva, snot and other such secretions. This can cause any number of problems, from choking to a type of pneumonia.

As I lay unconscious on the gurney, a nurse clamped a mask over my mouth for a couple of minutes to make sure I would have enough oxygen in my system while the attending team performed the intubation. After removing the mask, she tilted my head back as a young doctor approached with a hand-held device topped by a long, curved beak. The doctor opened my mouth, extending her first and third fingers like a pair of scissors to insert the smooth, dull blade of the laryngoscope on the right side of my mouth. She swept my tongue to the left and lifted it off the back of my throat to provide a clear view of my glottis and vocal cords. This in turn revealed the dull, wet, contextless flesh of Gigerian nightmare, ready to be invaded by a life-giving endotracheal tube.

The clear PVC tube was about one centimetre in diameter. A thin blue line of radio-opaque material running along its length was intended to make it more visible in a chest X-ray and gave it the appearance of a long, child's straw. To make it easier to pass through the curtain of vocal cords, and give the inserting physician a better view ahead of the tip, the end of the tube was bevelled. The doctor passed it just under a foot past my incisors and secured it at the corner of my mouth with surgical tape. The laryngoscope was withdrawn, an X-ray confirmed correct positioning of the tube, and the ventilator was attached. Now the tube could do its quiet work and wait for the moment its surprising length would be dragged out like a string of magician's handkerchiefs, lamprey mouth permanently agape.

I was spared a feeding tube. The official line was that this would not be necessary until a number of days had passed. Beth fretted that the decision was due to a medical conviction that I would be dead or unplugged soon enough in any event.

They measured my blood pressure three times, on three different monitors, because each time they thought the monitor was malfunctioning. No one could quite understand what exactly was going on, so I was rushed in for a CAT scan. While the resources of a major Brooklyn triage unit were being allocated to saving me, a man on the other side of the curtain was shouting his frustration that no one was attending to his mother. They'd been waiting a while. Mother hadn't been lucky enough to achieve a nine-in-ten chance of death, I guess.

In fact, apart from the 90 per cent likelihood of my impending death, our luck was holding up. As well as being lucky that Methodist was so close to our apartment, we were fortunate that, although I had just lost my job, I had been able to keep the health insurance I had maintained through my work. Healthcare in America relies on a system of hospitals mostly owned and operated by private business and paid for by private insurance. People aged under 67 get their health insurance either through their employer, or a family member's employer, with their premiums coming out of their pay each month; people on low income who meet certain other requirements are eligible to receive government help with medical costs. I was able to continue my insurance for an initial period of eighteen months pursuant to a statute commonly known as COBRA – so long as we could find the $769 a month to pay for it. At least for a while we didn't have to worry about, for example, me being denied new insurance coverage due to having a pre-existing condition – like, for example, the toddler who hit the news in the States when he was denied coverage for the pre-existing condition of being too fat. Or, you know, a toddler.

I had pretty decent coverage, too. Which was good, because Beth had enough to worry about without finding out, say, that after four days of treatment my insurance wasn't going to cover the costs and the bill was standing at $80,000. There was still going to be plenty of paperwork and co-payments and suchlike to take care of. It's hard to explain how forbidding the US healthcare system is to someone who's grown up with the NHS unless you've experienced it.

When the CAT scan was complete, the young doctor who had intubated me came out into the hallway to explain the situation to Beth. She was young and serious, with her long, dark hair pulled back into a bun.

'Beth? The scan has confirmed that Ricky has suffered a bleed in his brain.'

'Is that good or bad?' Beth asked, instantly wincing at how daft the question must sound. 'I mean, is that better than a clot?'

The young doctor explained the thing about clot-busting medication.

'So what do we need to do?'

'We're going to work on trying to get his blood pressure under control. The earliest we can schedule a procedure to reduce the pressure on his brain is 8a.m., after the surgical staff report for work. You need to rest.'

Beth wouldn't leave the hospital, so a nurse escorted her to a little waiting room. It wasn't a place made for sleeping. It was furnished with a short, two-seat, faux leather sofa. Beth curled herself up in it and started sending texts. She started with her best friend, a junior doctor. Dr Cowen to his patients, John to his fellow residents, and Sparky to his friends. Then she texted her mother.

In the morning, Sparky called for the latest news, and heard that I was due to enter surgery. Then he rang Beth's and his former flatmate, Mat, to tell him that he shouldn't expect to see me again. Beth's mother Kathy called back to make plans to come to Brooklyn. Beth felt guilty about that.

She felt guilty about that. She felt guilty about being alive. She felt guilty about the M&Ms she'd been eating from the hospital vending machine. She felt guilty about trying to get some sleep. She felt guilty about everything. She couldn't sleep. How could she sleep, while I was under the knife somewhere between life and death? Would she feel it, when I died? She scanned her mind, searching for a feeling that I was still there, or departed.

She felt neither.

Meanwhile, around nine hours had passed, during which my hair had been shaved and two holes had been drilled into my head, an inch or two above the hairline, each a couple of centimetres off the midline. The holes had punctured my skull, and a plastic tube had been inserted into each hole. The other end of each tube had been placed in a receptacle by the side of the bed, so that gravity could start to do its job. The process was similar to the siphoning that was involved in my father's home wine-making. The receiving containers had been checked, measured and recalibrated every hour, and the strength of the suck had been adjusted by changing the height of the containers. The big difference to home wine-making was that in that case, you're siphoning the good wine away from the sediment. In this case, the bad stuff – the sludgy mix of brain fluid and blood – was being removed *from* the brain. Also, they hadn't started the extra-ventricular drain by sucking on the other end.

There may have been other differences, too.

It was a relief for Beth when another doctor eventually came in, for a second at least. Then she remembered what he might be coming in to tell her.

'Miss Monahan?' He extended his hand. 'I'm Michael Ayad. We've finished Ricky's procedure.'

'And what procedure was that?' They were both sitting by now, and Beth fixed Doctor Ayad's eye. 'Why won't anyone tell me what's going on?'

Beth was lucky in the doctor she was talking to. Michael Ayad had a nerdy and vocational devotion to medicine, just like Sparky. He was the sort of doctor who credits his patients and their loved ones with enough intelligence to be able to process properly channelled information. In a pleasant voice – sonorous, with that hint of the South that suggests an appropriately unflappable attitude – he explained what had been happening for the past eight to ten hours.

The brain doesn't react well to a sudden influx of blood. One of its design flaws is that blood is an irritant to it. Blood gums things up. Meanwhile, the body continues to produce cerebrospinal fluid. 'A Coke can's worth of the stuff every day,' Ayad told Beth.

The body has to drain all this fluid somehow. It turned out that the projectile vomiting hadn't been some sort of fight or flight reaction, nor the nausea brought on by the sickening touch of the fingers of Death. No, the news was both better and worse than that.

I was experiencing increased intracranial pressure; a rise of pressure inside the skull. This can result in one of two events. The first is a midline shift, a shift of the brain past its centre line, which is A Bad Thing, because it's commonly associated with a distortion of the brain stem, which, in turn, can cause serious dysfunction. The second possible event, downward pressure on the brain, on the other hand, can cause death. This brain herniation puts extreme pressure on, and cuts off the blood supply to, various parts of the brain as one part of the brain is squeezed across structures within the skull. The pressure might even push your brain tissue down through the small opening in the skull near the brainstem, resulting in irreparable brainstem damage, paralysis, coma or death.

Beth decided that she would never look at one of those brain-shaped stress toys in the same way again.

'What happens now?' she asked.

'We wait.'

They waited.

Beth stayed all day, not least because she couldn't face going back to our apartment. Cole and Neal, a couple of friends from her business school, came round to express sympathy and disbelief. Eventually, Sparky drove over and he and Beth went back to the apartment, where he stripped the bed and cleaned up the mess. Then, while Beth fed and watered our cats, Seamus, impish Geronimo, and soft, shy, one-eyed Cyclops, he went to the airport to pick up her mother, Kathy Monahan, who had arrived from South Carolina to help fill the now vast and empty bed.

Beth would continue to look after the cats and continue the most basic level of maintenance of the flat, but would remember nothing of that. What had happened to us was all-consuming. Each morning before she went to work, Beth would cue up 'Classy Girls' by the Lumineers on her phone and walk the few blocks from our apartment to Methodist to sit by my bed and knit, or practice her needlepoint. It was all very homey, and the needlepoint was something she had had a yen to try for a while. She had picked up two beginners' kits. One picked out the words, *Don't Be A Dick*. The other read, *I Will Cut You*.

Yeah, Beth was a classy girl all right. It made sense that the Lumineers' track would be one of our songs; she even had a T-shirt she wore on our first date that described its wearer, in strategically ornate and illegible script, as *Fucking Classy*.

That first date had followed a series of chance encounters at Harry Boland's Pub, which Beth passed just three blocks to the west as she made her way to Methodist. I had given Harry's a wide berth when I first moved to the neighbourhood. With its name painted in a coagulated and curdled blood red above heavy black window shutters, Harry Boland's looked as though, were it in Edinburgh, it would have been the perfect place to go to get a good kicking. Harry's, however, turned out to be a quiet drinkers' pub that was open at whatever late-night hour I made it back from work. At my regular stool at the far left of the old, intricately carved bar, surveying the options thickly packed into the shelves of liquor, I could let the booze and the music from the jukebox wash over me, relax, and not worry about complicating a busy life by running into temptations of the flesh.

So it still feels a little ridiculous that even now, I can vividly picture the version of Beth Monahan who sat at the end of the bar at Harry's. Like me, she didn't want to deal with being hit on when all she really wanted was a Guinness and some time with her book away from her flatmates. Outside of this bar of hardened drinkers, that might have been difficult. Beneath her long, straight brunette hair and funky glasses, she would smile with her whole face. Lithe and slim, her jeans cleaved to her hips as perfectly as the shirt that outlined her small, jaunty breasts, and she moved with an alluring confidence and comfort in her body. She hated the attention that the accident of her beauty and the amused confidence of her intelligence drew. The word she hoped people would use to describe her was *irreverent*.

She had nothing to worry about from me, though. Her don't-bother-me vibes didn't have to work too hard to discourage a jaded guy in his mid-thirties from Scotland's famously repressed capital. There's a reason Danny Boyle had to turn to large cases of money and heroin addicts to get a few movies' worth of emotion and action out of the city of Edinburgh.

The bar was tended by Andy, a tall, slim guy who was missing a toe. Grinning beneath a mass of light brown hair, he had an air of Shaggy from Scooby Doo about him that belied a wicked sense of humour. Our bartender and mutual friend, he introduced Beth and I one evening in November. It was a work night, and we were the only three people in the bar.

'Do you guys know each other? C'mon, sit together. I think you'll get along.'

Andy probably just wanted to cut down on the time he was spending walking the length of the bar. Regardless, it turned out that despite an initial caginess, the intriguing, enchanting young woman and I couldn't help but get along. We discovered a shared passion for Scrabble and graphs representing the lyrics of rap songs. We began to play online games and email from time to time. After we had spent many hours over some weeks chatting in the bar, Beth sent me a Facebook quiz about herself. Playfully, to find out if I had been listening. Taking it, I discovered that she considered her long, smooth neck to be her best feature. Her guilty pleasure was a fondness for the movie *Die Hard*.

Our mutual attraction gradually began to assert itself. Like the sun, it was always there. It provided me with the light I needed to live, cooped up under fluorescence all day, every day, thousands of miles from my natural habitat. We couldn't look at it directly, though; after the failure of her first marriage, the young divorcée had decided that a long-term relationship was not for her. My marriage had fallen apart, too, and when I had visited a therapist to discuss the ensuing situational depression, she had asked what I wanted to do next. I had told her that I just wanted a nice little flat where Elizabeth would be comfortable visiting, and I could read my books and learn to play my guitar again – no complications.

Then Tall Jamie came for a visit.

Jamie was a friend of Beth's from South Carolina. She was matter-of-fact about sexual matters, and curious about what other folks got up to in the bedroom. When she visited Beth on her way home from a work trip to the north-east, they went to Harry Boland's together. That night, Beth and I chatted as usual, and when she went to the restroom, Jamie and I passed the time.

'Have you ever had a threesome?' she asked.

I hadn't. I didn't want one now. Not because I wasn't sure how the mechanics work so that one of the three isn't relegated to checking their Twitter feed on the phone, although I wasn't. Not because Jamie was unattractive; she wasn't. Not because I'd fallen for Beth and simply wanted to focus on the way her arms would wrap around me, and the painful pleasure of her nails tearing my back . . .

No, wait. That was exactly it.

I confessed to Tall Jamie my attraction to her friend, and she retreated, job done. A short while later, Beth and I found ourselves sitting on the wooden bench that faced away from the bar. It was hard and unforgiving. The ornamentation was minimal.

'You know,' I told her, 'this reminds me of the pews of my mother's church in Scotland.'

'Really? You don't strike me as the religious type.'

'I wasn't. I'd sit there in the front row of the balcony, thinking of my latest crush. Just like this.'

We both smiled, and our eyes locked, looking for confirmation. For the first time, we kissed.

Chemicals reacted, fireworks erupted, lights exploded.

On that casual first date when Beth wore her *Fucking Classy* T-shirt, I presented her with a crash course in single malt whiskies. She immediately graduated to Laphroaig and other smoky Islays.

'It tastes of salt and sea and sex,' she declared, and I abandoned the sweetness of my former Speyside favourites for something more complex.

We discussed the circuitous routes that brought us to New York City. She, by the escape pod of business school after her parents had moved her as a sixteen-year-old from Rhode Island to South Carolina, and she had become an accountant after studying at the University of South Carolina. Me, via a series of exchanges and scholarships that had led to a decision to spend a couple of years in the city, ten years, a million dreams and a young daughter ago.

We played darts together. I found out about her geeky interest in the NYC subway system. We wandered late-night streets after forgetting coats at parties. She discovered my obsession with downbeat British pop music. We picked up temporary tattoos of black hearts at a local coffee shop together.

One night, as we lay in bed, Beth told me about the time her former marriage counsellor had shared her own strategy for dating. The counsellor hadn't wanted to waste time on relationships that didn't have the potential to last, so she asked potential suitors a series of questions to separate the wheat from the chaff. Beth had come up with her own set, and shared them with me. Would I consider having another child? This was something I hadn't previously considered, but the answer was suddenly obvious. With the right person, of course I would.

Would I contemplate raising that child as a vegetarian? Again, the answer was 'Yes'. The ideal version of me that was buried deep inside the hard-nosed financial lawyer who ate whatever he could pick up at his desk before getting a couple of hours respite at the bar and starting again didn't want to eat meat. He wanted to be better in so many ways.

A month later, we were walking from the bar to Beth's apartment when she gave me a meaningful look. 'You know what I love?' she asked.

My heart didn't have room to beat in my chest. It squeezed up through my throat to catch a glimpse of the woman who was causing adrenalin to flood my body.

'Grapefruit juice.'

She smiled, and I knew what she meant. Things were moving quickly, and a girl and boy each with a failed marriage behind them were too canny to say it yet.

I could only reply, with enthusiasm, 'Me too. I love grape-fruit juice, too.'

The exchange of signals was clear, and a week later, we were back at Harry's again, choosing tunes together at the jukebox. I sat on the counter, a low wooden dividing wall that jutted into the bar space on the right of the jukie. Beth nestled between my knees. Our eye-beams twisted, and threaded our eyes upon one double string. I could see her thinking, weighing her words.

I knew it was a leap, a gamble, so I made an announcement. 'I'll say it,' I said. Then because I knew, and because I wanted to help and make it OK, I continued: 'I love you.'

The narrator of 'Classy Girls' would have said that the hardest part was through. On that clear, springtime Brooklyn night, I might even have agreed with him.

3

The Valley of the Shadow of Death

The intensive care unit at Methodist Hospital was as pleasantly sterile an environment as the ER was on a good day. Wide corridors were floored in peaceful combinations of sky blue, cream and cinnamon. There was one nurse to every two patients, each of whom was allocated their own room. Mostly, the patients were quiet, being too unconscious and hooked up to too many machines to kick up too much of a fuss.

All day Monday and Tuesday after my brain surgery, the drains in my skull quietly did their job and I regained a type of consciousness, although I wasn't yet able to create memories. On Wednesday, the medical team let me start to wake up and took out my breathing tube. This was a big step, because breathing tubes are very vexing, and the possibility of me trying to pull mine out had been a big concern.

Although the breathing tube had been removed, alien tubes still emerged from my body at all angles. As well as the two tubes that were inserted into my skull, an arterial line had been inserted into the radial artery in each of my wrists, to constantly monitor that pesky blood pressure. It was still worryingly high. A line was put in my left wrist first. Then, later, it was changed to my right. I also had a regular blood pressure cuff, a kind of line that could provide intravenous access over a prolonged period of time, and leads on my chest for an ECG. As well as all that, the same day as the breathing tube was removed, I was fitted with a Foley catheter.

A Foley catheter is a diabolical and complex thing, but in simple terms, it involves running a tube up the patient's urethra and into the bladder. After insertion, a balloon on the inside end of the tube is inflated with water to keep the catheter in place. Once my Foley had been inserted, the first of what the doctors called the activities of daily living could begin, and I could take the first steps out of the valley of the shadow of death.

Soon after the breathing tube was removed, my doctors declared that the most important thing now was to get me eating. A swallowing test was quickly administered. As Beth looked on, a speech pathologist came to my bedside. She checked the suction apparatus on the wall for use in case of aspiration, then she raised the bed, presented me with a viscous solution, and asked me to swallow. This was followed by a glass of water, more challenging because water is more difficult to detect for a throat numbed by stroke. Each time I swallowed, the pathologist would feel my throat to check that the reflex was in order.

'Well done!' she said, after each swallow. 'How did that feel?'

It felt fine, and I was allowed to begin eating again. Or so I thought. Shortly after the swallowing test, a nurse brought the first item of solid food that was to pass my lips after the stroke, and placed it on the table that slid over the heavy bed.

I registered a piece of bread. Not exciting, but something. I trustingly took a bite.

The soft, wet substance in my mouth had neither the consistency nor the taste of bread.

'What is this?' I spat at the nurse.

'It's bread.'

'No it's not, it's Soylent Green!'

This was a sharp, instinctual response. Beth, looking on, was surprised to find herself laughing out loud. In these early days, she was particularly worried about my confused state. Then, without missing a beat, this reference was interjected with the confident delivery of the sharply dressed lawyer who had died at the end of September. Years later, I've still not seen the 1973 movie *Soylent Green*, about a future in which the population of a dilapidated New York City survives on green wafers supposedly containing high-energy plankton. But I had absorbed enough pop culture to know that *Soylent Green is people!*

Of course, this limp offering wasn't people-food. Nor was it food for people. A little water had been added to some bread, and the mixture pureed per guidelines 'to have the look and texture of pudding or mousse'. Most of the sustenance that was now being provided to me was appetising to the same extent.

Nevertheless, I had now started to take on limited amounts of food and water. Between the stroke and all the tubes, I couldn't get out of bed. One day, not long after I had woken up, Beth and Kathy were sitting quietly with me when an anguished look passed over my face.

'I need to pee!' I told them.

'It's OK,' Beth said. 'Just go.'

'What? Here in bed?'

'Yes. Go ahead.'

The Foley catheter did its job. There was a long list of risks associated with its use, though. Among the most severe was that the patient may pull out the catheter while the balloon holding it in place is inflated. This can lead to what is delicately referred to as 'major complications or death', particularly when the patient is mentally impaired. After all that had happened, I certainly qualified for that description.

When Beth and Kathy left, I started to try to pull the Foley out.

Shortly after this incident, the Foley was removed, and I was fitted with a series of Texas, or condom, catheters for the remainder of my stay at Methodist Hospital. I learned that a stroke and the related pain and numbness did not lend themselves to the state of magnificence for which a condom is manufactured. I complained to Beth about the constant readjustment the catheters required.

'I feel like my penis is under incessant threat.'

Beth decided against expressing her amazement that my vocabulary seemed to be intact, and tried to reassure me. 'Baby, your penis is fine.'

'OK. Then you should keep it in your mouth at all times, just to make sure.'

We were discovering that a common symptom of brain injury is acting or speaking inappropriately and impulsively. Because stroke patients tend to behave inappropriately and impulsively, the nurses had me wearing mitts. As a very premature baby, I had worn little mittens, because I couldn't be allowed to scratch my delicate skin. As a thirty-eight-year-old whose brain was open to the elements, I couldn't be allowed to touch pretty much anything. I hated those mitts, and from time to time, could be found lying in bed gazing uncomprehendingly at them, trying to figure out what the hell had happened to me.

Yet somehow, through all this, the extra ventricular drains continued to work. This was great, because it was important to get me out of intensive care and into rehabilitation as quickly as possible. Research shows an association between earlier admission to intensive rehabilitation and better outcomes for haemorrhagic stroke victims. This is particularly the case for the most severely impaired patients. Patients like me.

Then, on Thursday, one of the drains stopped working. It was clogged with the sticky mixture of cerebrospinal fluid and blood, which is some pretty crappy wine in anyone's language. Although they entered on different sides of my head, the two tubes drained out of the same place so it wasn't a massive problem if one of them stopped working. Except, it's like a plane: if one engine goes down, you can limp home on the other. If that second engine fails, limping is the least of your worries.

To compound the problem, I went on to pull the dressing off my head one night in a sweaty, sticky state of uncomprehending agitation and ruined the sterility of the tubes.

The doctors took out the blocked tube. The remaining tube worked through the Monday a week after surgery. Then I became lethargic. Almost unresponsive. Admittedly, it would have been hard for most people to notice any difference, what with the brain injury and all. However, put together with the fact that the drain hadn't produced any wine for a good hour or so, the signs weren't good.

I was taken for another CAT scan. The scan showed that the remaining tube had moved four centimetres out from where it needed to be, and the medical staff couldn't just go ramming that now non-sterile tube back into my brain.

There were two options. They could remove the non-sterile, disgusting, germ-infested tube and put in a new sterile drain. Or, they could put in a lumbar drain. This had the dual benefits of being a somewhat less delicate procedure, and also leaving me with a type of artificial appendage that I was less likely to pull out.

Without wanting to blind you with science, to put in a lumbar drain, the doctor punches a hole in the patient and runs in a plastic tube. So far, so much like the other drains. Except this time, instead of pushing a plastic tube into my skull, the doctor pushed the tube up the inside of my spinal column. Instead of using gravity, the tube was connected to a burette and a drainage bag. A nurse would come by every hour, open up the tap, and drain a specified amount of the fluid into the bag.

If the lumbar drain worked, the doctors would be able to think about moving me to the intensive care step-down unit. Thankfully, it did work, but I was kept in intensive care for a further week because whatever they did, they couldn't get my blood pressure down to an acceptable level.

The problem with all these wee plastic tubes was that, while they had solved the immediate problem, I couldn't have them in me forever. Eventually, it would have to be established whether my brain could start regulating the cerebrospinal fluid on its own, so the doctors had to challenge the drain. Well, they said 'challenge'. They meant, 'switch it off for twenty-four hours'. Meanwhile, the nurses would watch for symptoms that might show fluid was building up. As well as lethargy, these symptoms could include headaches, and – of course – death. So, the spigot was switched off.

Pretty quickly, I started leaking fluid out of my back. This, Beth was told, constituted a fail on the test. Given that it seemed I couldn't drain my brain on my own, the alternative was to put in a shunt – in this case, a kind of valve – which would stay in permanently and drain the cerebrospinal fluid as necessary.

This would require more brain surgery. A foreign object inside my head. More risk of infection. A delay in getting into rehabilitation. Dr Ayad didn't have any slots to operate before Monday morning, though, so there was time to do a second test. Second tests aren't unusual, but I wouldn't have had one otherwise.

On Friday, my spigot was turned off again. This time, there was no leakage, and no sign of headaches, lethargy or death, so a CAT scan was scheduled for Saturday morning to determine the success, or otherwise, of the test. It showed a slight enlargement in my temporal horns. Although that's a brilliantly sci-fi sounding name, temporal horns are merely the part of the lateral ventricle extending downward and forward into the medial part of the temporal lobe. Or, to put it another way, imagine you've sliced a cauliflower in half. Now, imagine you find a hole in the cauliflower shaped a little like an inverted comma or a horn. That's kind of what a temporal horn looks like. It's part of the ventricular system of cavities in the brain where the cerebrospinal fluid that bathes and cushions the brain is produced. This enlargement in my temporal horns wasn't sufficient to indicate a failed test. Moreover, I was still responsive. So, the lumbar drain remained switched off. On Sunday I was still fine, and the drain was removed. There wasn't even any call for a follow-up CAT scan.

This was great news! There was no need for further brain surgery, with the associated four-day recovery before I could be moved into rehab at the Rusk Institute in Manhattan. Rusk had been designated as the best rehabilitation programme in New York and one of the top ten in the United States since rankings began.

I had received some therapies at this stage, but these mostly involved being helped out of bed to sit in a chair so I wouldn't get bedsores. Not at all like the intensive rehabilitation I could receive after my immediate medical issues had been resolved. Now that my body was regulating my cranial pressure and cerebrospinal fluid, and my blood pressure was under a degree of control, the worst of my medical issues were addressed and the success of my recovery was all down to repairing the damage to my body in rehab.

I was moved to the step-down unit, where four beds separated by comfortingly pastel curtains in primrose, sage and terracotta were monitored by a nurse at a long desk. As a precarious passage to the outside world began to open, I was granted a window with a view north over urban arboretums across the restrained Brooklyn skyline to the unmistakably phallic Williamsburgh Savings Bank Tower. This view was wasted on me, of course. I was in no condition to check it out. Nevertheless, even in my reduced state, I couldn't leave my friends at Methodist Hospital without one final dose of drama.

For whatever reason, the arterial line in my wrist bugged the hell out of me. I was damned if I wasn't going to do something about it, mitts or no mitts. By the time I had been moved to the step-down unit, the equipment was no longer available for the arterial lines to display the continual blood pressure reading. My friend Kirk visited, and was troubled by the scene that confronted him. After they had sat by my bed for an hour or so, Beth walked him to the corridor. Kirk was another Scottish lawyer living in Park Slope, and we had first bonded at a kids' birthday party over a shared love of depressive pop music. Now, just a few years later, I lay prone in a hospital ward, an intimation that maybe there weren't better times ahead. A warning that working hard, obeying authority and doing the right thing didn't necessarily bring its own rewards

'Are you OK?' Beth asked.

'Yeah, I'm fine,' said Kirk. 'But forget about me. How are you?'

'Just got to keep going for now,' she shrugged.

'And then what? For how long?'

'We don't know. All we can do is wait and see.'

A meaningful look passed between them.

'Is he . . . When is he coming back?'

'We don't know. He might not. Not the same way, anyway.'

One of the nurses walked by, and smiled.

Kirk stopped her. 'Why haven't you taken that line out of his wrist? Can you not see how agitated he is?'

She told him it would be removed in the morning.

When Beth arrived before 8a.m. the next day, she was told that I had had a rough night. This was not unusual. Although the step-down unit had those lovely views, the ICU had no windows, and my body clock had been broken by the time I had spent there. I would sleep through Beth's visits and lie agitatedly awake through the night. I think I have a memory from that particular night of feeling that malaria-carrying mosquitos were attacking my wrist. It makes a little sense that I might have been thinking that, given my abnormal posturing, occasional sweats and the fact of that hallucinatory idea itself. I thought that weakly murmuring pathetic requests for help would be the best way to get some assistance with my plight. However, when it turned out my pleas were too weak and pathetic to generate any assistance, I had to take matters into my own hands. I suppose that I must have been showing some signs of lucidity during the day, because I was mitt-free.

I tore the arterial line out of my wrist.

That was a terrible idea. There's a reason people pull a nice bath, pour a bottle of wine and slit their wrists, and it isn't because they've seen a vision of their girlfriend's beautiful eyes while walking through a Scottish garden, and are desperate to live. No, if you pull out your arterial line, you can die. Fortunately for me, a nurse was standing over me when it happened and was able to immediately apply pressure. Maria had to do this for a full five minutes, praying that when she released her grip I wouldn't bleed out. There was a lot of praying to be done in that time, not to mention time for the nurse to reflect that if she couldn't stop the bleeding, I'd have suffered a fitting punishment for the shit she'd have to go through in the aftermath. Time to reflect that she didn't really mean that. So she just continued to apply pressure, because only a minute had passed.

Eventually a second minute passed. A third, finally. Another nurse came by, and Maria asked her to quickly bring a bandage. When the other nurse brought it, she gingerly eased off her grip and immediately applied the bandage, very tightly. When it was all done, she held my hand.

'You're a very lucky boy,' she told me.

I was certainly happy that the mosquitos had stopped and that someone was taking care of me, holding my hand. I even submitted to being re-mitted and wrapped in thick sleeve dressings.

It was clearly way past time for me to be moved to Rusk, where they would have the time and skills to teach me to think straight again. Not that it would take me long to get put back on a 24-hour watch.

4

Frankenstorm

My transfer to Rusk took place on a Wednesday, three and a half weeks after the stroke. It was an afternoon. Beth had come in to Methodist for her morning visit, and would come to see me in my new home in the evening. Having made a brief trip over, my father made a final visit the next day before heading back to Scotland on Friday. In one sense, the worst was over. In another, it was just beginning. My friends were concerned that the Ricky they knew was never coming back.

Storm clouds were gathering over New York.

The medical centres that make up the Rusk Institute are scattered around the city. An ambulance took me to the Hospital for Joint Diseases, or HJD, at Second Avenue and 17th Street in Manhattan. A grey monolith, its entrance was plunged into darkness by a canopy of blue plywood scaffolding. A large, silver truck would sit outside every day, unmoving, the doors to the main compartment plastered with ominous warning signs.

Inside the hospital, the corridors of the ninth floor were lined by long, blue counters facing wards accommodating pairs of patients. Nurses sat facing the open doors of the wards so that the stroke patients and other victims of brain injuries who had somehow managed to avoid being put on 24-hour watch could still be monitored. The nurses were lovely, and their faces would burst into life when they were providing encouragement to patients. Unfortunately for them, they spent most of their days dealing with people who couldn't understand what was going on, or what had happened to land them in this place. When you catch a glimpse of a nurse, unaware, at one of the long blue counters, you can see the toll it takes.

It didn't help that, at the time of my admittance, HJD was being renovated. Although the wards themselves, with their shiny, polished blue floors, were spick and span, the corridors were lined with mysterious items of hospital equipment. Thick polythene sheets draped along the hallways made the shapes of things blurry and indistinct. The elevators moved slowly. The voices of late-night visitors and the pleas of the stricken floated through the scenes of dilapidation. Despite the efforts of the staff, there was something phantasmagoric about the scene, mirroring as it did the disarray and confusion in the minds of the patients.

I was moved into a two-man ward with a man named Alfonso Dallier. My first memory of Alfonso is that of meeting someone I already knew. I still had little handle on the passing of time, and memories still tended not to stick. Alfonso was memorable, though. Originally from Mali, he had subsequently spent a number of years in Haiti. Of possibly advanced but indeterminate age, his face was chiselled but not harsh, bobbling above a wiry frame. He was at his impish best flirting with the nurses, or scooting down the halls, gown flapping and tiny wee bum peeking out. With his carers in hot pursuit, he looked like nothing so much as the mischievous Calvin from *Calvin and Hobbes*, if Calvin was an eighty-something-year-old stroke victim.

More often, Alfonso was in a heightened state of fury. He was furious about people who came into the room backwards. 'He can't come in like that!' he would yell.

He was furious about people getting his age wrong. To make matters worse, it seemed that no one could figure out from his records exactly how old he was. 'I'm not eighty-three! I'm eighty-two!'

He was furious when I kept my light on at night. 'Make him switch it off!' Being scared of the dark, he was equally furious about all the lights being switched off. 'Switch the light back on!'

He was especially furious when people wouldn't attend to his constant demands.

'Help me! I'm not dead yet!'

'Well, no, mate,' I would mutter to myself. 'I can tell that by the bloody racket you're making.'

In fact, Alfonso could rage about anything. Over the course of a single morning, his rants could run from the state of the US healthcare system to the location of his pants. Which was a wide canvas. Despite all that, the first clear memory I have of Alfonso is not of his belligerent face contorted with rage, but the face of a scared old man.

My first proper memory of Alfonso is one of the first memories I managed to make after my stroke.

Having spent most of three and a half weeks in bed, and many of the nights fretting and perseverating, I would often wake during the night. Perseveration is a phenomenon I would never have been aware of if I hadn't had a stroke. It means the repetition or prolonging of an action, thought or utterance after the stimulus that prompted it has ceased, and it's an important word in this story.

On this particular night, I was free of the condom catheter and awoke with a need to use the toilet. While I knew I was in the hospital as I began to create this new memory, I was too discombobulated to remember that I had suffered a stroke that had paralysed my left side.

I pushed myself up, somehow, with a view to making my way to the toilet, wherever that was. I got, maybe, two steps across the room before Alfonso's terrified face sped up at me from his bed. Good old Alfonso, though. He might have been scared of the dark, but in the face of ten stone of Scotsman crashing onto his elderly frame in the middle of the night, he located his panic button, and the nurses arrived in no time to get me back to bed.

The 24-hour watch was resumed.

From that moment on, I had a certain affection for Alfonso, notwithstanding his ornery nature. In my mind, I cordially christened him 'The Wee Man'. For all his intransigence, Alfonso wasn't a bad bloke. He prided himself on being a 'church man', who was 'in the choir'. Although, oddly enough, when he got the Sunday service on the telly, it seemed pretty clear that even I'd make a better fist of 'Christ Is My Saviour', the twenty years separating me from Wardie Parish Church and my express bus ticket to hell for being a securitisation lawyer who had torpedoed his marriage notwithstanding.

By the time I was transferred to the Hospital for Joint Diseases, it had become evident to Beth that the irreverence she so valued would be the key to us getting out of this storm together. For better or worse, she had tied herself to the mast of my ship. Otherwise, there was nothing to stop her from walking away. Nothing except love and the memory of the man she had been dating at the end of September.

What do you do when the person you're with is destroyed? Because make no mistake, for the time being, I had been destroyed. If a man is the collection of his memories, I had been erased.

At Methodist, I would be asked, not just every day, but with every change of shift, the usual set of questions for the victim of a brain injury. Things like, 'What's your name?' and 'How old are you?'

Most days, I knew who I was. On one day, I asked a passing resident doctor for some ice chips. 'Get me some ice chips! I'm a very important man. I'm going to be the vice president!'

'Of what?'

'Of the country, man! What do you think?'

Getting my age right was always difficult. My stroke had occurred two weeks after my birthday, and that hadn't been enough time for my new age to take. I was like someone writing the wrong date on his cheques after the turn of the year.

As well as not being quite sure when I was, I couldn't say where I was. One day, a resident doctor stood at the end of my bed and asked the usual questions. Beth sat in a hard plastic bucket seat, biting her nails and wincing with every enquiry.

'Do you know where you are?'

My eyes skittered back and forth as I scanned the empty space in my head. I threw out a guess. 'A school?'

'No. Can you try again?'

'A building?' I'd given up. I just wanted this to be over.

The doctor persevered. 'What kind of building?'

'An office building?'

Beth tried to help. 'Have a look around.'

I had a look around. Oh my god. 'Am I in a hospital?'

'Yes. You're in hospital. Do you know why you're here?'

My eyes moistened. 'Oh, crap. Have I had another stroke?'

'No, Lover,' Beth reassured me. 'Just the one.'

On one of our last nights out before the stroke, Beth and I had gone to a storytelling night in Brooklyn. The host, a guy called Peter Aguero, told a story about his wife, a woman with epilepsy. After she has a seizure there's a thirty-minute period during which she's like a computer rebooting. Every single time, he's convinced that this is it, and he's never going to see her again. That wherever she goes when she has the seizure, she's never going to come back. Beth had a similar experience with me. I would bounce between good days and bad, and my mental presence would wax and wane like a sine curve, but less predictably. She worried that my recovery would be less like a computer rebooting, and more like our bloody awful cable box. I'd just sit there, stuck at some useless point, able to identify her as 'my friend and helper', but not able to recall what we always liked to call 'Our Thing'.

34

I did refer to Beth as my friend and helper one day. In my mind, it was meant to be sweet. She was my best friend. I wanted to acknowledge, without becoming too maudlin, how much I appreciated everything she was doing for me, but it just made her feel a little sad and scared. I only found out about that some time afterwards, because it's difficult to gently communicate with a stroke patient. Whereas Our Thing was constant communication. Crashing weddings for free gin. Call and response in-jokes. Charming strangers as a couple in bars.

In the short years, the too short years, leading up to my stroke, Beth and I would separately listen to a sex and relationships advice podcast each week. Maybe on the commute to work or on the train back to Harry's to play in the darts league or at the office desk, eating lunch. Then we'd sit on the balcony of our apartment to smoke and dissect that week's calls and the host's responses. Dan Savage would often return to his theory that there is no such thing as a soul mate. That there is no such thing as The One, but there are The Ones. What there is, is someone close enough to The One that we can make a decision to round them up.

It was a theory that appealed to the rational romantics on the balcony. The dissection was good practice to instil the openness and confirm the compatibility our relationship needed. Sitting on our balcony before The Event, the warm glow generated by and for eight million souls cast across the red brick turrets of the 14th Regiment Armory opposite, Beth and I had reflected on what would become of us if our romance ended. We each speculated that we would return to our original post-failed marriage lives. For me, a string of increasingly infrequent affairs, each more melancholy than the last, as the shadow cast by the loss of the love of my life lengthened. She would return to her independent life, offering herself to a gay friend as a surrogate to satisfy any maternal urge. We would get by.

Now, having half-glimpsed the possibility of a wee, bobble-headed, half-Scottish toddler one night in bed not so many months ago, Beth walked along the side of our apartment building, listening to the Lumineers on her way to get the subway to HJD. While the fulfilment of our daydreams seemed less likely, the alternative scenarios looked less tolerable. So, somehow, when she would get to the hospital, we would cling on to our daydreams. We would talk about opening a distillery in the Highlands. Incredibly, Beth had written in her diary, on Day Seven, *I think it might be a really good idea.*

As far-fetched as they must have seemed at this juncture, these conversations helped us. We managed to maintain pleasant chats about the next post-recovery steps in our relationship. We discovered that's important for a couple recovering from a stroke. The dreams and aspirations that do so much to sustain a relationship can be drowned in the blood and shit and tears and snot of the harsh reality of a stroke. It was good to remember from time to time that a partnership is for better, as well as for worse.

As we chatted on the first Sunday after my transfer to HJD, Beth told me that everyone in the city was talking about the impending arrival of the hurricane that the media, and even the government, would soon nickname *Superstorm Sandy.* Sandy had started with a tropical wave in the Caribbean six days earlier, on Monday. By the time the weekend came around, awareness of the approaching storm had permeated the therapeutic bubble that cocooned HJD's patients. The staff talked about it and swapped the news they had heard, and the hospital's plans, with their friends at other institutions. On the wall at the far end of my bed, CNN ran on a TV at the end of a hinged, black metal arm.

They were talking about a *Frankenstorm.* The term was meant to evoke the joining of Hurricane Sandy with a second storm front as it approached the east coast, to create a monster storm. As I lay crippled in bed, watching the news describe the six different levels of evacuation threat being allocated to New York neighbourhoods, the word grabbed me roughly by my delicate neural circuits.

Certainly, as Sandy approached New York, she appeared increasingly monstrous. My experience of storm scares in the north-east had been that they would be talked up before blowing themselves out just off the coast. This time, the news reports talked of Sandy barrelling north-west towards New Jersey. This time, she did. As Sandy smashed into Jersey, there was speculation that she would push a wall of water into New York Harbor. The coastline around New York Harbor channelled the water that Sandy was blowing from the Atlantic into the city and into a narrower and narrower region. Because New York is mostly at or below sea level, includes large swathes of reclaimed land and is set within a coastline of bays, inlets and funnels, the threat was all the worse.

As hour after hour of immaculately coifed, interchangeable anchors gleefully celebrated the fact that there was some real news to report, the rise of the waters in New York Harbor and the Gowanus Canal was mirrored by the rise of the anxiety in the topography of my brain. Throughout my stays in Methodist and Rusk, I was often agitated, and when this agitation descended, the nurses would hail Beth's arrival. When I saw her arrive, whatever was going on would blow away like a *cumulus humilis*, and a sunny smile would emerge as I exclaimed, 'Oh hi, Baby!'

On the night of Sunday, 28th October, the day before Sandy's arrival in the city, the Metropolitan Transport Authority shut down the city's subway system. Beth left the office and went to Union Market to pick up some groceries before hunkering down. The experts were predicting that Sandy would sit over the metropolitan area for two or three days once she hit. They advised the populace to batten down the hatches, get supplies in, and prepare for the science that kept New York City running to be battered into the stone age. The city's electricity would be going down, we were warned. Cell phone coverage would fail.

By Monday, the storm had settled in the city like an ageing Scottish hipster and wasn't going anywhere. The Breezy Point neighbourhood of Queens was ablaze, after rising sea water flooded the electrics of a home in the area. One hundred and twenty-two homes were destroyed in that neighbourhood alone. The news was apocalyptic. Intrepid reporters stood on the Jersey Shore, being pelted by the waves pouring over the boardwalk. The Gowanus, just six blocks down the Park Slope from our apartment, and one of the most contaminated bodies of water in the United States, poured over its banks and into homes.

Then there was a massive phosphoric flash at the ConEd substation on 14th Street at the FDR Highway in Manhattan, clearly visible from across the river in Brooklyn. The blast looked deafening to the Brooklynites, even though nothing could be heard over the roar of the wind. A transformer had been flooded, and the resulting explosion knocked out power below Midtown. Liquid had compromised the city and destroyed its functionality.

Up on 57th Street, a 150-foot crane boom flapped to and fro in the winds, twisted and crumpled, uncontrollable, like a stroke patient's weak arm. Reporters worriedly admitted that nobody knew if the damaged limb could be brought under control before disaster struck, and it plunged a thousand feet onto a gas main. The power outages extended to Langone Medical Center at First Avenue at 30th Street on the East Side, where nurses were carrying newborns down nine flights of stairs so they could be transferred to a location with power.

At HJD, the backup generator was operational, but no non-essential lights were operating. The two patients in Room 920, addled by the unfamiliarity of their situation, even before Sandy hit, were plunged into their own personal Bedlam. Poor Alfonso, scared of the dark, demanded that power be restored.

My mind raced in perpetual, uncontrolled disquiet, and I begged to be allowed to use a phone. In the face of my ranting neighbour, I just needed to talk to my girlfriend, the nice girl with the brown hair and the glasses. She was clever and brave. She could persuade the staff to let me go home into her soothing embrace.

The problem was, the phones didn't work. I couldn't call Beth. She couldn't call me, and couldn't get any information online. For the only day during my stays a Methodist and HJD, she couldn't visit me, and I was lost. Unable for the most part to create new memories, I was without the anchor who tethered me to the frightening world outside. I was without the person who, as confused and out of time as I was, triggered something that made me smile whenever she walked into the room. That one day stretched and stretched, and without the ability to gauge the passing of time, the prospect of getting out and going home seemed to recede. Without Beth's reassuring presence, the idea of going home suddenly didn't seem any less frightening than lying in a hospital bed as the storm raged over the city.

At last, Sandy relented, and the city haltingly checked the extent of the destruction, and what was working. By Tuesday evening, Beth's fellow citizens were still in their homes and the roads were empty. She got a lift into town from Sparky, the ideal man for this job. An ear, nose and throat doctor, with a talent for facial reconstruction surgery, he was unflappable. With a banana suit in the trunk, he had the requisite irreverence. Besides, because he worked a hundred hours a week, he was prone to falling asleep at the wheel and crashing, so empty streets were a good thing.

When they arrived, Beth and Sparky found me still awake, with the rattled Alfonso and our 24-hour watch nurse for company. Sparky had to get back to Brooklyn, so they weren't able to stay for long, in the dark. Still, the easy familiarity of Beth and her best pal was a salve after two days during which I had been plagued by terrible angels standing upon the sea and the earth, clothed in dark clouds, their feet as pillars of fire, their voices roaring like thunder along the claustrophobic Downtown streets.

I still wanted to go home. Beth could only promise to come back the next day.

By Wednesday, downtown New York had spent days in darkness. The staff at HJD couldn't regulate the patients' body clocks with electric light. The city outside, though, was slowly coming back to life. Beth was expected back at work, even though her office in the Financial District would be out of commission for six weeks. The foyer of the building conveyed the solidity and affluence of the typical late twentieth century financial cathedral while eschewing ostentatious flash, as required by tradition. A lustrous marble floor escorted the slap of leather brogues and the click of office heels past multiple security desks to various banks of elevators and escalators that ferried masters of the universe and peons up to the offices and cubicles above and down to the Dunkin' Donuts and the dry cleaner's below. In a world that was working properly, there would be no need to leave the building to attend to sustenance or hygiene.

On this day, the scene downstairs resembled something from a post-apocalyptic movie. The cleaner's and the doughnut chain store were completely submerged in floodwaters that reached the top of the basement stairs. Similar scenes were replicated across New York. There would be no power in the East Village for the rest of the week. The subways remained inert. Of course, even an act of god couldn't stop the gears of finance, so Beth had to report for work at another office in Brooklyn. At least that was a little more local. The MTA had decreed that city buses would be free on Wednesday and Thursday. With everyone going back to work, the subway down and the city's petrol stations dry, the three-mile trip from 15th Street took two hours.

At least it made for a shorter work day. Beth made it home to get ready to visit her stroke bloke, having arranged a lift from one of our Boland's darts team buddies, Matt. Fortunately, they had enough gas to make it to the hospital. Unfortunately, New York City was the world's biggest stroke patient.

It's generally known that, if you have a stroke on one side of your brain, the opposite side of your body will be the weak side. I had never seen it said, though, that if the stroke patient draws a line directly down the centre of himself, the delineation between the two sides is quite exact. One of the most worrying moments of my convalescence was waking up one morning, rubbing my eyes, and feeling the numbness in my left eye and eye socket. It felt like my stroke would surely have some effect on my vision. What else could be affected? I scanned the rest of my body, doing an inventory. My two nostrils felt quite different, and would do for some months. Not noticeably, most of the time, but certainly if I had a good dig around. That was even though they're right in the centre of my head, and right next to each other.

I continued down. The two sides of my rib cage felt different, that was obvious. However, the difference was even perceptible when I touched the edges of my breastbone with the fingers of my good hand. Further down, I was amazed to discover that, slightly but perceptibly, even my two testicles felt different.

An iconic photograph covering *New York Magazine* in Sandy's aftermath painted Manhattan in a similar light. Or, at least, parts of the city were in light. The view, from the south-west of the southern tip of the island, showed the Williamsburg Bridge, over which Beth and I had gleefully ridden on the Malaguti weeks earlier, lit on the Brooklyn side, but with the lights abruptly dying halfway across the

East River. A sharp diagonal line, running from 39th Street on the East Side to 26th Street on the West Side, separated those with power to the north from those in darkness below. Battery Park City, to the south of the island, but just north of the Financial District, was illuminated. To the north of Battery Park City, coated in Teflon, blazing like a beacon of Freedom – or, as the political blog *Roadkill Refugee* tweeted at the time, '*a giant middle finger to the rest of New York*' – stood the Goldman Sachs Tower.

When Matt and Beth had finished navigating the empty streets, unlit by street lamps or traffic lights, and reached HJD, they found that, like Goldman, it was running on its backup generator, at least to the extent of vital services. The lights in the corridors were on. Life support systems and monitors provided the only radiance in the wards.

Room 920 was in Cimmerian shade. Notwithstanding his fear of the dark, Alfonso slept. In light of the anxiety the storm had generated, and the absence of any distracting activities, I had also suspended my consciousness. The scene on the ninth floor was even more eerie and ominous than usual, and my visitors stayed just long enough to pick up my latest batch of pee-soaked clothes.

Outside, New Yorkers had just about had enough of this storm bullshit, and regardless of any Armageddon, were beginning to get on with their lives again. Together with the imperatives of global capitalism in its Babylonian capital requiring that everybody get back to work and then, perhaps, figure out some way to get home, this meant that the trip home to Brooklyn took two hours.

Then something poetic happened.

5

For Whom the Bell Tolls

On Thursday, 1st November, power was restored to Lower Manhattan. That afternoon, the lights went back on at HJD and, with pleasing symmetry, the lights went back on in my head.

Up to this point, my visitors had been worried about whether there was any Ricky left. The lights weren't on and there was nobody home. Or if there was, he was rattling around in there like Miss Havisham.

The life-threatening danger appeared to have passed, but the sack of muscle, fat, bones, nerves and blood lying in one of Room 920's beds displayed none of the distinguishing characteristics of the human being formerly known as Ricky. My studiedly mussed hair, the symbol of the well-to-do Brit around New York, had been shaved in the style of an inmate of Bedlam. I had lost 35lb in the aftermath of my stroke, even though Beth was regularly bringing me cream puffs the size of Sonny Liston's fist, our love packed into tasty symbols of intensity and pleasure. I responded to basic stimuli, but my lawyerly garrulousness had largely evaporated. Although there had been an amusing ridiculousness to my uninhibited verbal flailings, the intellectual underpinnings of a properly absurd sense of humour had been extinguished.

Core functions, like an automatic politeness, continued, but I spent much of my time sitting in bed staring at a bunch of flowers, or my shit-covered hands, or whatever other object had recently been magicked into existence. Without a functioning memory, nothing had any context. No day had any relation to any other day. No event had any connection to any other event. Life was simply a procession of serially managed occurrences. Any advances in rehabilitation were meaningless beyond the encouraging words of my therapists, because I had no idea how things had gone the previous day. I was broken today, just as I had been broken yesterday, and would be broken again tomorrow. I was a goldfish. Except goldfish have memory spans that can extend to five months.

Beth would come in after work and ask if my friend Jonathan had visited that afternoon. I would reply, no, I hadn't seen him, even though he had been in just an hour or two earlier. With no ability to form a narrative to shape the events of my life, I bobbed loosely in a sea of unconnected faces and events. I was always happy and grateful to receive visitors, but unable to gauge who these people were, and what their visits meant.

In almost two months, Jonathan was the only work colleague to visit me in hospital. The other men and women for whom I had generated millions of dollars of fees, who had called themselves my friends, whom I had considered friends, never once appeared. Sure, the firm had let me go, but where was the humanity?

One of these colleagues had been shot in a botched mugging in the early nineties. His heart had stopped on the operating table. Twice. On each anniversary of his shooting, he had held a deathday party. For a few years, anyway. Then he no longer had time. The three thousand billable hours a year he logged required over eight hours of billable work a day, every day, three hundred and sixty-five days a year. That was just *billable* time. Add an hour of billing and collection. Half an hour for each of breakfast, lunch and dinner. A couple of hours of drafting, negotiation, review and research written off each day, to keep the client happy. Another couple of hours reading the legal journals and periodicals relevant to one's field. An hour of continuing legal education, preparing presentations or training associates, depending on the day. Two more hours wining and dining, or otherwise sucking up to clients. The government recommends half an hour of moderate exercise daily, and seven to eight hours of sleep. That's twenty-five hours, so clearly urination, defecation and fornication are out of the question – never mind visiting the sick. He didn't have the time to be alive.

Thinking of him made me ask myself: if I was ever able to recover, would I ever be able to return to the only thing I had ever been trained to do? And would I *want* to? That life didn't seem like much of a recovery, or much of a reason for a party.

I have wondered if the absence of visits from my colleagues was related to a lawyerly conservatism, particularly given the proximity of my collapse to my layoff. I was never a litigator, always a transactional lawyer. Nevertheless, for anyone immersed in a world of adversarial positions and risk aversion, the perils of a visit to a former employee who had, until recently, worked these sorts of hours would have been clear. Particularly if any sympathy was expressed by the visiting party. *I'm sorry you're totally fucked*, is a little too close to, *I'm sorry we've totally fucked you*, even if I never saw it that way.

Although I never saw it that way with respect to my situation, there does seem to be something wrong with the world of corporate finance. Ten and a half months after my brain exploded, a twenty-one-year-old intern at Bank of America Merrill Lynch in London worked three nights in a row. Early each morning, he would pop home for a quick shower while his taxi waited outside, before returning to the office. This ritual was so commonplace in London's financial houses that it had a name: the Magic Roundabout. In the environment in which I had worked, three nights in a row wouldn't provoke much in the way of comment. Moritz Erhardt, the intern, was eventually found dead on the floor of the shower cubicle of his temporary accommodation. A subsequent inquest found that he had died of an epileptic seizure, and that while fatigue could have been a trigger, that couldn't be said for sure. I think about Moritz Erhardt a lot.

Working in a grotesque monument to urban brutalism in Midtown, I didn't have the luxury of a magic roundabout. My office had a window, at least, but it was still a grim little space, unleavened by my attempts to provide personal colour. When I first moved into the office, the firm arranged to have their picture hanger come by and hang my two reproductions of Edinburgh scenes. I would see them as I entered my office each morning (assuming I left the night before), but never took a second to look at the view along Princes Street towards the Scott Monument, or the convivial but conscientious constable directing traffic at the bottom of the Mound. A print from the Philadelphia Museum of Art dominated the wall facing my desk. An early seventeenth century Japanese scroll by Hon'ami Kōetsu, it sparsely, almost abstractly, depicted an impression of a silver river running under a sky washed in gold. In the foreground, a poem card bisected the horizon. I meant for Kōetsu's piece to inspire a mindful contemplation amidst the crowding in of conference calls, drafting and review. Ten years on, even before my stroke, I couldn't remember a line of the poem.

The lines of the calligraphy fell from the sky, dissolving into the river below, a shakiness in the penmanship showing that the piece was completed after Kōetsu began to suffer from slight palsy.

> A mountain temple
> Evening and the sunset bell,
> Whose every voicing
> Vibrates with a message sad to hear:
> 'Today too is over, dusk has come.'

46

I love the image I've painted in my mind of Kōetsu sitting in the valley as the mist rolls down from the hilltops, his brush trembling as he continues his project of presenting the verses of the *Wakan roeishū*. The days are slipping by, but the artist must let the river carry them away.

In my office a few blocks north of the simple, functional lines of Lever House on 53rd Street, dusk would fall, but the day would never end. Each parcel of twenty-four hours merged seamlessly into the last, and the petty pace crept from day to day, to the last syllable of recorded time. Tomorrow never came. The lawyers would be the people the bankers would call to keep the candle burning when they had called it a night. I would emulate the example of my bosses, and, if they were working at 5a.m., or their couches were covered with the work of the day when my drafting was completed at 6.30a.m., I'd find the tiny area of my little office floor that wasn't covered with discarded drafts from the prior year, or three years, or ten years, and lie down on the grotty carpet, inaccessible to the cleaner's vacuum, for an hour's sleep.

The firm my ex-wife had worked for when we moved to Manhattan boasted a gym, shower facilities and accounts with the best restaurants in town, not because their associates deserved to be treated like royalty, but for the same reason that the dry cleaner's and the doughnut shop had found the basement of the building of Beth's employer a profitable location: it was best if the more junior members of the team didn't have to go home to wash their clothes or eat a proper meal.

When I reached the Hospital for Joint Diseases, my visitors were mostly from outwith that world. An ex-girlfriend, Jenny, got a message to me to ask if she could visit. Our affair had mostly been conducted in her apartment, in a dark crevice off Manhattan's side streets. Another hard-working young attorney, she nevertheless couldn't afford a place near to her office that would allow in more light, or for that matter, had much in the way of walls or doors – it was basically a bedsit described in more aspirational terms. Just thirty short blocks from where Lever House cast a damning shadow over my place of work on Park Avenue, we drank wine in a flat that embodied the way that ideals of modernism had been perverted in cities around the world.

Lever House is a thin, floating and visually light vertical glass slab evocative of the alien beauty of Kubrick's monoliths in 2001, but built in the International Style advocated by Mies van der Rohe. As such, it evokes a design process in which rational thought is employed to achieve spiritual goals. The city-dwelling pedestrian passes an open plaza featuring a garden and pedestrian walkways. The tenant has use of a building designed to reduce operating and maintenance costs, and keep out the grime of the city.

Where I worked, on the other hand, was a building so ugly and unsuited to purpose that it would soon be demolished because it no longer met the requirements of a modern office building. Its windows were separated by unsightly white brick, and its only characterising feature was a slavish adherence to the old city zoning laws requiring setbacks from the street as the building clambered into the sky.

Jenny and I had been joined by our unhappiness over the courses our respective lives had taken. As I had emerged into the lighter climes, I had withdrawn from her in a fashion that I had hoped was kind, but on reflection was neglectful. I subsequently discovered that, some time after our affair ended, she had suffered a nasty injury requiring hospitalisation. Given my conduct and her penchant for melodrama, I did not anticipate her visit with relish, but merely hoped that it might be an opportunity for healing.

Lying in bed with little to occupy my mind now that Sandy had passed, I considered what made a good hospital visit. In its essence, visiting an inpatient is a selfless deed. A distaste for hospitals, and their imagined stench of cleaning supplies, sickness and death, is enough to discourage many people from visits, unless they are infrequent and required by guilt. At the same time, it seemed to me that the last thing the broken, confused inhabitants of the neurological ward needed were visits in which the visitor exuded a backslapping self-congratulation. Why, I wondered, would people who had written you off now want to co-opt your drama into their story?

I was contemplating all this when Jenny arrived in the ward and took a seat.

'Hi. How are you doing?' She laughed. 'Stupid question, right?'

'Not really. I'm feeling . . .' I stopped, and actually tried to answer the question. 'I'm feeling pretty positive, I think. Pretty upbeat. It's better than working in a law office, right?'

I think that we were both relieved at how easily we had managed to pick up a conversation.

'I don't know. That's a pretty extreme way to take some time off.' She smiled again. 'It's funny. For some reason I had been thinking about you and the time we spent together before I heard what had happened. It's a shame things got complicated at the end. We kind of stopped communication on a negative note, didn't we?'

We did. We had drifted apart, and the last time we had caught up, I had fallen in love with Beth.

'It was good to hear from you,' I told her. 'I'm sorry about the way things ended. I suppose a lot of that time was pretty dark for me. I'm sorry if my issues led to me being careless. I mean, I know they did.'

I filled her in on the rough outline of what had been going on with me, and she told me that not a lot had changed with her, but she was doing OK. We passed a pleasant hour, and I was glad of the company. When she got up to leave, we didn't make any plans to meet. To her immense credit, Jenny's visit was a thoughtful and enjoyable one that left me feeling much better at its end than I had at the beginning. She was solicitous, open and comfortable, and I was happy to find her in a better place.

In fact, if the aim of a hospital visit is to leave the convalescent party in an improved state, then I have to say that the vast majority of my visitors were exemplary. They were patient and, as befits an appealingly intellectually curious group, interested in my condition, while not dwelling too heavily on the hazards on the road ahead.

There was a great deal of concern shown for my primary caregiver, too. Many friends asked Beth if there was anything they could do to help. A kind thought, and one that is helpful in providing the warming knowledge that one's friends care. When the caregiver is frazzled by daily pre-work visits, though, as well as the coordinating of a trip through a storm-ravaged city to drudge in an unsympathetic workplace before returning to the hospital in the evening to pick up piss-soaked clothes for laundering that night, it's a question that's too open-ended to easily answer.

It turns out the most helpful thing to do was make a specific offer of help to the caregiver. The most supportive questions were ones like:

'I'm coming round for a visit. Can I bring you something to eat?' or 'I'm going to pick up some groceries. Can I take you along? Or get you some essentials?' Or one that sticks in my mind even though I didn't hear it: 'Are there any TV shows or movies you've been wanting to watch? I could bring you some box sets.'

Maybe it's the monotony, or the blank walls, but there's something about a long hospital stay that intensifies the reaction to any art that's available. My first hospital stay I can remember with any clarity was at the age of twelve, for appendicitis. I probably struggled on with stomach discomfort longer than I should have, because I had a schoolboy ticket to see Scotland play France at rugby on the Saturday of that week. By the time I was checked into Edinburgh's

Western General Hospital, my appendix was fit to burst, and my parents were told that just another couple of hours could have been fatal. Just like in every other appendicitis story. I will say this, though: the pain was even more intense than the endless, savagely beaten pain of my stroke.

I say, 'remember with clarity', but most of what happened during the period of my appendectomy had slid into Kōetsu's silver river and been carried through the mists of the Ishikawa prefecture, beyond my view. But I do remember the video for U2's 'With or Without You' on *Top of the Pops* on the Thursday evening following my surgery. It never ceases to transport me to a bed in an NHS ward at the far end from the door, perpendicular to a window looking over springtime Edinburgh, with a wall-mounted 1980s television nearby. Even now, why it should stick with me seems obvious. The video was striking, all stark black and white. What was the driving cause, though, was the very reason that the band's manager was against releasing it as a single, and why Adam Clayton thought it sounded more church than radio – it was sonically *unusual*.

Five years later, when I was in my final year of high school, another group of orderlies were wheeling me around Edinburgh's old Princess Margaret Rose Hospital with a herniated disc. The first thing I remember from that hospitalisation was my best friend of the time coming round with a bag of fresh cherries. I'd only had maraschino cherries before, and these mysterious, aubergine-coloured things were a revelation. The second thing I remember was a volume of the complete works of Oscar Wilde. I think I'd borrowed it from the library before being confined to bed, but it was in hospital that I plunged into it and devoured it alongside every juicy cherry in a couple of sittings before discarding them both by the side of the bed, sated.

By the time of my stroke, medical professionals had cottoned on to the beneficial impact of art on the convalescent. At

Rusk, we had the benefit of a recreational therapist, Dawn. A birdlike, friendly and solicitous woman with short hair, Dawn would bring art and therapy dogs to Room 920 and watch us interact with them from the far end of our beds, near the door. Experienced in handling Alfonso, she was ready to lob a couple of sarcastic ripostes from a safe distance. A safe distance from the two stroke patients being a span even shorter than the very few yards to the door. One day, she brought a jazz guitarist to the wards. I don't really remember much about him, other than his virtuosity. Dawn introduced the strokey odd couple to the guitarist, attempting to play up our credentials as a receptive audience.

'This is Alfonso. He's from Mali. He's a church man. He sings in the choir.'

I didn't remember making any such definitive identifying statements about myself, and wondered how Dawn would describe me in a couple of strokes. As of the end of September, I wasn't a practicing lawyer. I hadn't yet looked into the future to see whether I would be again.

'And this is Ricky. He's . . . a Scottish hipster.'

Jazzman wasn't fazed, he just put the data into the jazz-puter in his head. Either it had a really fast processor, or he just decided to play what he played for all the broken people. A bit of both, I think, because the choices worked, and for whatever reason, seemed appropriate. Something by Steely Dan, followed by 'Georgia', which I came to discover is the hospital musicians' standard.

On another day, Dawn brought around a young singer-songwriter called Aly Tadros. Born in Laredo, Turkey, Aly was just twenty-five at the time, but had visited Turkey, Spain and Egypt, and had the open, agreeable manner of the young traveller. Her long, dark hair and musical style hinted at an exotic background. Hers wasn't a name I recognised, but when she played a short set of covers and originals, I made a point of noting it. When she was done, I tweeted into the real world: '*Wonderful performance by Aly Tadros in my room at HJD. I encourage you all to have a stroke, to see her in such intimate surroundings.*'

Much later, I discovered that Aly had also volunteered with care communities in Austin, Texas, and regularly played at hospitals, retirement centres and assisted-living homes, including as part of the Musicians On Call programme.

Some of the musical talent I was exposed to was more home-grown. I was surprised one afternoon to see Beth come into the ward with our friends J and Gregg. Surprised, because I didn't know them *that* well. I think my longest meeting with Gregg had been a brief introduction when Beth and I had gone to see a DJ set by Jake Shears of the Scissor Sisters at the Hayden Planetarium on the Upper West Side. J, I knew a little better, having met him on a number of occasions when I escorted Beth to events hosted by the business school. I'd even been to his flat once. It had been another bizarre mishmash of spaces that somehow formed a young New Yorker's apartment. At this point, though, my most vivid memory of him was standing on the roof of a converted church, sharing a pack of Parliaments while we tried to help him with his relationship concerns. Beth had, after all, written an occasional column of relationship advice for the business school's newspaper.

It was the sort of vaguely drunken meeting during which all the participants connect and have a sense that we could all be good, long-lasting friends, and try to silence the nagging voice suggesting 'Maybe at a different time; we're all terribly busy; my friend roster is pretty full'. Nevertheless, leaning against the brick of the tiny lean-to that emerged from the flat roof, looking out over the jumble of the Lower East Side, J's unaffected sincerity and our genuine concern had been enough to form a connection. And now, here he was.

My surprise was only heightened when, beyond the hospital-issue sheets, in the fall light coming through the sealed window, Gregg – or Nappy Pipes, to give him his name on the decks – carefully removed an alto sax from its case, and the lads politely asked Alfonso if he would mind if they put on a show for their ailing acquaintance. As well as polite, this request was sufficiently bizarre that The Wee Man had no context in which to balk, and blithely acquiesced.

So it was that a hip, skinny, Jewish MBA student transformed into his alter ego, Mouthmatics. A studio-quality version of the introduction to 'Billie Jean' emerged from somewhere inside J. Twenty-nine seconds introducing an iconic bassline that Quincy Jones attempted to cut from the song before Michael Jackson objected because that was 'the jelly – that's what makes me want to dance'. Now I was getting to experience it live, in my sterile little cabin of ill health.

I couldn't dance, as much as I wanted to. It was still an effort to get myself into the bedside chair. As the nurses gathered and bobbed in the doorway, though, I felt the rhythm move me, and the happiness igniting my broad smile saturated me. Beth and I had spoken recently of dancing, and I would recall the tiny, sweaty Scottish clubs of my youth, and the sort of whitewashed cube, stuffed with revellers, to which I had threatened to escort her for these past few years. For now, that was another daydream.

We spent a good amount of time daydreaming during my recovery. Groping along the walls of the dark tunnel of recovery, not knowing what monster is around the next bend, we had to reach for the light. Future day trips to St Kilda and flowers, as much as puncture wounds to the groin and angiograms. Beth wrote me a note in hospital one day, echoing an ambition I had expressed to a physical therapist – 'I can't wait to go running in the park with you.'

In fact, Beth would often scribble a message on a Post-it note to leave on my sturdy over-bed table. The table was a beast of a thing, with four long skinny feet extending from a single, sturdy, and oddly grotesque leg. The feet ran on four straining castors, so the table could move over and retreat from my bed throughout the duration of my stay. It was a breakfast table, work surface, lunch table, reading desk and dinner table. A billboard, too.

The first note Beth stuck to the table read: 'This is only temporary.' It was a thought expressed to her by a nurse while I was still in Methodist, and it became our mantra. An article of faith for the patient and the carer. Seeing it stuck to my hospital table each day helped me get through the day. Beth would come in before work and after work, and be reminded that her task was not – hopefully – Sisyphean. She was encouraged to pen more notes.

'I hope you feel incredibly loved.'

'Stay focused so you can come home soon.'

As the two-inch squares expanded along the edge of the table, people began to take notice. After a few friends had commented on how much they liked the notes, visitors were invited to leave remarks.

'Better than dead!' wrote Sparky.

'You now have a valid excuse for "forgetting" to wear pants!' came from Beth's other flatmate, Mat.

Our friend Paul's wife Jen offered, 'Your stroke weight-loss program was a raging success!' Elizabeth wrote, 'You are a cool Daddy! I ♥ you!'

Beth's notes were already beginning to reflect advances. We had moved from the general and hopeful 'This is only temporary' through 'There's no crying in rehab!' to the whimsical 'Maybe you'll be ambidextrous' and 'Don't choke on anything today,' reflecting weakness on my dominant left side and the resurrection of irreverence.

We hadn't reached 'Let's go four to the floor with Francois K at Cielo,' however. We weren't going clubbing any time soon. The dancing would have to come to us. Much to our surprise, it did.

The corridors at HJD reflected the cost of real estate in Manhattan. Use was squeezed out of every available square foot. While the corridors were wide, the outer walls were arrayed with idle equipment. The inner edges of the corridors were lined with those long nurses' workstations, and between the equipment and the workstations was where the tango took place.

Not between the classy girl and the cripple, of course. No, Dawn had brought two young students from the storied Juilliard School for the performing arts on the Upper West Side for our entertainment and edification. Patients who were interested and able lined whatever wall space was left, standing, leaning on walkers and sitting in wheelchairs, and after a brief demonstration, our performers related details of the origin and development of the dance, as well as expanding into explanations of the nature of modern dance and choreography. Their passion for the passionate dance, and dance in general, imbued the often dead-eyed denizens of the brain injury wards with enthusiasm. The diversion was completed with a full demonstration. The dancers displayed their expertise by tangoing up and down the four-foot width of available corridor. Somehow, they managed to move from the very close embrace necessitated by the styles that emerged in crowded Argentinian dance halls into flashes of open embrace that allowed the display of complicated footwork and flair.

As the embrace opened, the narrow corridor spread. Eventually, it expanded to encompass a whole world of possibilities.

We'll do that one day, I thought.

6

The Shit Doesn't Hit the Fan

Each day, one of my doctors would come round to check on my latest status. Occasionally it was Doctor Blum, the neurology professor who was the titular head of my case. She passed by with such impressive efficiency that my sub-goldfish brain hardly registered her role in my recovery, never mind her serious haircut.

On other days, it was Doctor Karp who dropped by. A specialist in internal medicine, his areas of expertise included post-op evaluation and preventative medicine. All high forehead, glasses and beard, he wasn't one for small talk, and I found it hard to warm to him. As time passed, it emerged why he tended to be in a state of heightened frustration when we spoke: Doctor Karp had drawn the short straw of selecting and calibrating the medication required to keep my blood pressure at safe levels, and nothing seemed to be working.

Most often, I was interviewed by Doctor Im. A physiatrist, or rehabilitation physician, he had a mysterious battery of tests that he ran through on each visit. Each check-in began with a casual chat.

'How are you doing?' Doctor Im would ask.

'Not too bad, I guess.'

'Did you sleep well?'

'It took me a while to drift off, but I suppose so.'

That sort of thing. Except, these chats weren't so casual.

As we talked, he was inspecting my face and looking for any asymmetry.

Then, Doctor Im would take my hand and flick the tip of my middle or ring finger. From time to time, he'd have a resident or two with him, and they would get the chance to have a go. I would always assume that it was simply some sort of test of the functioning of my extremities, and that if my middle finger snapped back, everything was in good shape. All of Doctor Im's residents had studied hard, though, and when their boss asked them to check for Hoffmann's, they would flick my fingers, but watch my thumb. My thumb would flex in, and everyone would agree that I was demonstrating Hoffmann's reflex. Nobody seemed overly concerned about this, and I had jumped to my incorrect own conclusion, so I didn't learn until well after I had checked out that Hoffmann's reflex is indicative of problems in the area of the brain that conducts impulses from the brain to the spinal cord.

Doctor Im always asked me to smile, too. This one seemed pretty obvious. He was looking to see whether my smile was symmetrical, after the havoc that had been wrought in the right hemisphere of my brain.

It wasn't. I didn't realise that, and anyway, this was always one of my favourite parts of the day.

The doctor would lean over me and direct me to, 'Smile. Like this.' Then he would display the cutest smile you could imagine, like a four-year-old playing up to the camera.

Next he would say, 'Puff out your cheeks. Like this.'

It was all I could do not to reach out and playfully pinch his adorable four-year-old's cheeks. Finally, each examination ended the same way. It didn't matter if it was Doctor Blum, Doctor Karp or Doctor Im; they would ask 'Have you moved your bowels today?'

Then they would ask, 'Are you having any continence issues?'

It became apparent that the staff of HJD were more obsessed with toilet habits than the cast of a 1970s British comedy. Each day, I would answer the continence question in the negative, with increasing frustration.

Eventually, I began to ask, 'Why do they keep asking me that?'

The nurses and residents, and even the doctors asking the question, were very circumspect. 'It's just a question we ask everyone,' they would say. Or, 'They just want to know how you're doing.'

It took the woman I trusted most, the woman who didn't have to worry about how I would react, to explain. I asked my question, and the eyes that brought me back to life narrowed behind her spectacles. My jokes weren't usually quite this deadpan and bleak, even now.

'Are you serious?'

'Yeah. I've got no I idea. I feel like they're treating me like a toddler.'

'Do you remember when I came in to pick up your piss-soaked clothes?'

I was lamentably aware that the feeling on my left-hand side was dead, other than to the dread discomfort arising from the pressure of any hard item. What I hadn't noticed was the internal deadening. This was nothing metaphysical, you understand. I corporeally couldn't feel parts of my insides. Though this internal tactile demise started at my left nostril, it burrowed into me and made me wonder why my heart, to the left of my centre axis, hadn't been paralysed, too. The deadness screwed right down to above my pelvic floor, and the little elastic sac that sits there.

I wasn't totally numbed to the feeling of wanting to urinate, but when I did notice it, it was usually at such an advanced stage that I had to desperately ask for the grey collection bottle that was kept by the side of the bed. The body of the receptacle was a flat rectangular box that could lie on the mattress during use, its receiving spout slanted upwards, with rounded corners and sharp seams where the moulding met on the side. If I wanted to take a shit, I asked for one of the stippled cardboard bowls in a darker shade of grey. The involved process of manoeuvring over the bowl, under the sheets, wasn't the most empowering action, but at this point filling the bowl and keeping the sheets pristine was the kind of small victory I would have to take.

I tried not to feel too bad about the indignity of it all. Everyone has to expel their waste. This was where the staff's interest in our procedures became useful. Not only because of the basic need for the patients to avoid soiling themselves, their clothes and their beds, but because, since there are so few things the recovering stroke patient can, or particularly wants, to do for themselves, using the bathroom is the first action that can be used as a learning tool.

One of the most important things I had to learn was to adjust to my new inabilities, like a reverse Spiderman. A simple task like making my way to the lavatory was fraught with peril. I couldn't just hop out of bed and stroll over to the toilet, as Alfonso and I had learned. It turned out that this was a useful lesson, as one of the greatest dangers of relapse for a stroke patient is trying to do too much and taking a fall. From this point on I was more cognisant of my deficits and didn't attempt to do too much on my own.

Room 920 had its own en suite toilet. A palatial thing, it could easily be a spare bedroom in Jenny's or J's apartment, or the apartment Beth and I shared. You could even swing a cat in it, or an unwieldy wheelchair. With grab bars lining the walls that led to a throne elevated high enough to facilitate transfer on and off, it was a pleasure to spend time there. But it might as well have been in one of the outer boroughs. It was all the way over by the door to the room. My bed was on the opposite side, and I was separated from the prospect of relief by tables, the trek along the aisle between the two beds, and a left towards the door, before embarking on the long haul to the Promised Land.

I was under strict instructions not to undertake this journey alone. My fall was the stuff of legend on the ninth floor, so each nurse would begin her shift with a warning to me that I was not to attempt to get out of bed alone, but was instead to press the call button on the bulky handset attached to my bed.

I had to press that button a lot.

Each morning, a nurse would bring me a tiny plastic cup containing the cocktail Doctor Karp concocted for me like a master mixologist. The pills changed from time to time as he fought to stop the blood coursing through my blood vessels with such dangerous pressure. Nevertheless, there were two constants in the cocktail. There was always a diuretic to encourage my body to get rid of any excess salt that might elevate my blood pressure, and a big, red gel cap that looked like an oversized, translucent jelly bean. In my confusion, it looked like the taste of strawberry fondant, and its soft, yielding wall encouraged me to pop it with my teeth.

It did not taste of strawberry fondant.

The gel cap was a laxative, and although the taste of the thick scarlet substance that oozed over my lips was noxious, its effect was quite glorious. I would press the big red button and be loaded into the big, solid-state hospital issue wheelchair, so as to be wheeled across the vast expanse of the ward, dotted with its unexpected hazards. Before long, when I was out of my gown and allowed to wear pyjama bottoms, I was taught how to most safely and efficiently pull these and any underwear down, using a procedure that involved bracing my legs against the clothing to keep it within easy reach for retrieval. When my modesty was restored – or if I experienced any difficulties – I was to pull the thin red cord hanging by the wall to the side of the toilet so as to be escorted back to bed.

61

Between deposit and pick up, I would sit on the elevated seat of the toilet, and my insides would fall into the bowl below. I was entirely evacuated. It wasn't as unpleasant as it sounds. I would emerge lighter, and with a sense of accomplishment. In fact, I came to look forward to my little visits. I wonder now what Freud would have made of Alfonso and I, and our odd toilet habits: he, holding on to his little rocks of poo even though they tormented his insides; me, relishing the next opportunity for relief. The rebellious little Calvin, who required everything be ordered to his satisfaction, and the messy Scot, who wanted to share things with his peers but could be inconsiderate of the feelings of others. Who needed to learn about controlling his behaviours and urges.

In fact, my expulsions felt less Freudian than Zen. A letting go, a moving on. I was filled with an empty space, leaving room for the next moment.

Months later, when my bladder was under control, I could walk into a bathroom ready to urinate like a regular guy. No panic, no drama. Then, as soon as I clapped eyes on the toilet in the corner, the desperate urge would rise, like a swelling river threatening its banks, or a thundering waterfall or the crest of a crashing tsunami. The internal numbness must still have been present at that point, though I wouldn't have known.

A year after the banks of that blood vessel in my brain broke, I went to a movie at a local cinema. As befitted a successful art house theatre, the cinephiles could buy their tickets in a breezy atrium from young enthusiasts sitting behind an open desk, and accessible toilets were readily available. So much so that I found myself in one when I was simply looking for a regular gents' lavatory. Once, this room would have conveyed a certain dolour, with its extra space for the walker or chair, and the grab bars lining the walls. Now, standing in front of the toilet, I saw that thin red emergency cord and a different feeling washed over me. I was comforted. It was the red string of Rachel, the favourite wife of the biblical Jacob, a protective segula. I was reminded of the kindness of my nurses, doctors and therapists. I thought of the words of the rabbi who wrote that the red string recalls the merits of consideration, compassion and selfless-ness, and that it is a reflection upon this, and the inspiration to good deeds, more than the string itself, that might protect me from harm.

As I reflected upon the alarm cord, I saw that life was good and that I was surrounded by kindness. My left leg was still gimpy, but I had let my former life go, without judge-ment or regret.

7

Hot Shower Action

Beth's favourite motivational Post-it note read, 'Sean Connery is the poor man's you.' Thirteen days after the power came back on at HJD, I wheeled out my impression of James Bond and Goldfinger for the first time in two months for the entertainment of one of my nurses. Sally had figured out that the best way to compel my cooperation was to appeal to the conscious, deliberate cheer I was beginning to cultivate. A small, young, Asian-American woman, she usually took the early morning shift. She would walk into the quiet ward after Alfonso and I had finished our breakfasts, and a booming, twenty-stone Scotsman would emerge from deep within her tiny frame.

'Urr ye rready furr yerr injection, Misturr Brroowwn?'

She had studied in Edinburgh, so her talent for Celtic mimicry put my ten-year-old daughter and my girlfriend of almost three years to shame. Elizabeth's attempts would veer into Julie Andrews as Mary Poppins territory, and Beth's apery would take a stroll underneath the arches into the East End of London. More 'Gor blimey, Myeree Poppins,' than Julie Andrews as Mary Poppins. By now, she refused to even tackle a burr, sticking to a well-practiced Billy Bragg imitation.

I had talking like a Scotsman down like a pro, though. Caught in this bed, in this strange place, as a long, thin, blood-thinning needle was prepared to puncture my abdomen just like it was every morning, I was James Bond, strapped to a cutting table as an industrial laser approached my most delicate parts. I smiled insouciantly.

'Sho, Goldfinger. Do you eckshpect me to talk?' Then I skipped into sinister, gold-smuggler mode as Sally giggled. 'No, Mister Bond. I expect you to *die*.'

I told Beth about this later in the day, terribly proud of myself. From somewhere in the dark corridors of my long-term memory, where the emergency generators hummed on while my short-term memory was sunk under Gowanus waters, I had been concerned about something called foreign accent syndrome. It's a rare medical condition that the newspapers love to report on. It arises most often after stroke, and it describes a patient appearing to develop a foreign accent. They don't. The appearance is simply the result of distorted articulatory planning and coordination processes.

Of course, that's not as funny, is it?

'Do you remember that Goldfinger bit I used to do at Boland's when I was trying to make you laugh? I did it for one of the nurses this morning. I was relieved it didn't sound like Roger Moore and Christopher Walken.'

Beth turned round to our friend Joe, who had accompanied her that morning. 'Oh my god! Can you imagine if he'd woken up with an English accent? He'd be in hell!'

Despite my best attempts to speak more slowly, and trying to enunciate more clearly, Americans from Texas to Pennsylvania had failed to understand me over the past decade and a half, even if New Yorkers, living in one of the gooiest, fondue-iest part of the melting pot, hadn't had the same problem. When I had first moved to Austin, Texas to study, I had experienced particular difficulties ordering pizza by phone. My elongated vowels were a different shape to those of the South, and since this made it almost impossible to pronounce my own surname comprehensibly for a drawling Texan, my attempts to provide the deliveryman with some kind of guiding context had led to pizzas being delivered for *James* Brown. I would yelp with soul at the door so they wouldn't take the pie away.

When I later moved to Pennsylvania, clinging to the possibly apocryphal claim that Invernessians speak the clearest and most melodious English anywhere in the world, and noting that Edinburgh is considerably closer to Inverness than Philadelphia, I would get quite upset about the natives' inability to understand me. I concluded that the average American would hear a foreign accent and simply switch off. For some time, in protest at this laziness and enforcement of cultural imperialism, I gave up trying.

Eventually, though my accent remained stubbornly Scots, my vocabulary migrated west. Rubbish bins became trash cans. Elastoplasts, Bandaids. Trousers were pants and pants were underwear. Eventually, my 't's ceased to be glottal stops, then mutated into 'd's. I lost track of where my accent had landed. Somewhere in the middle of the Atlantic, though definitely more Rockall than Nova Scotia. It had ceased to be important.

Though blunted, my Scottishness wasn't unimportant. Meeting the particular person who becomes the love of one's life is statistically unlikely. We could meet another love of our life, another person who brings out that something within us. But that specific person? What were the odds that the vision in the tweedy blazer at Boland's bar who had just wanted to be left alone would want to take up with me? Remote, I would have thought, except . . .

Beth was born on Burns' Night, the birthday of Scotland's favourite son, the Ploughman Poet. Her first boyfriend was a Scot with the name of a member of New Order – and when you're from Rhode Island, Macclesfield's close enough, right? Her parents' longest-standing friends were the Scottish parents of that boyfriend. Her ex-husband was actually named Robert Burns.

Not that she was looking for a life of shortbread tins and skirling pipes, which was just as well. When I was first attempting to broaden my horizons, I had applied for a scholarship from the St Andrew's Society in Edinburgh. I got through the first round before finding myself sitting in a dark, stony room in the basement of Edinburgh's Old College, before a panel of four dark, stony men.

'What does Scotland mean to you?' the third, impassive, slate suit asked.

I feigned reflection for a moment before delivering the answer that I thought would mark me out from the other serious young men and women.

'Social justice and hardcore techno,' I replied

That marked me out, all right. Dead air echoed through the room. The formerly impassive countenances of the firing squad arrayed on the other side of the long, dark, wooden table collapsed into the ashen, apoplectic faces of pirates presented with the Black Spot of the law school's alumnus, Robert Louis Stevenson. I would have to find a more congenial benefactor to finance my move to the States.

What Beth found in her Scotsman, strangely enough, was an affirmation of the best parts of being American. When I lapsed too far into Hobbesian paternalism during our balcony chats, she would propound a Jeffersonian individualism. She championed forthrightness and an embracing of emotion that would have shaken the high hedges of the Edinburgh neighbourhood where I was raised. The petrifying stoicism of the city of my child-hood that had enclosed me like dragonhide slowly began to erode.

Not long after my mother had passed away, Beth was out of town, and I went to The Rock Shop on Fourth Avenue in Brooklyn. I had a ticket to see another Edinburgher, Edwyn Collins. My life had become a disastrously unsustainable misbalancing of work, regrets, love and grief.

I was only peripherally aware of Edwyn's health concerns, so it was a shock to see Grace, his wife and manager, lead him across the stage to his position behind the mic. Then his band powered into an inspired mix of post-punk and northern soul, and the long, thin venue collapsed into an even more claustrophobic corridor of smiling, dancing fans. The physicality of the music in the tiny hall compelled me to join the politely flailing mass of limbs, and before I knew it I was dancing like a maniac and sobbing uncontrollably.

This articulate, extravagantly-quiffed man, forever young due to his founding of the Glaswegian band Orange Juice and the legendary Postcard Records, had been ravaged by stroke. My tears weren't sad, though. I was delighted to witness his Scottish two fingers to his situation, rocking and painting and fighting back with sheer willpower and the help of his family. Even his reliance on a silver-topped cane was an act of defiance; the dandyism of Baudelaire, close to spirituality and stoicism.

This strength came from the love he shared with his family: Grace and their son, William. When he suffered aphasia in the wake of his cerebral haemorrhage, the singer with the dark chocolate baritone was able to repeat only four phrases: 'Yes', 'No', 'The possibilities are endless', and Grace Maxwell's name. Resonating with my parents' background in Glasgow and Paisley, and my time growing up in Edinburgh, it was a beautiful and inspiring night. I was reminded that with humour and joy and love and popular music and pride, the possibilities were, indeed, endless. I was able to grieve for my mother at last, and found myself re-invigorated to fight for a better future. Edwyn would have been able to tell me that the time for tears, and the exaggerated changes in mood of the stroke survivor, had not even yet arrived.

The time for tears still hadn't arrived when I was in HJD. I wanted to cry whenever I dwelt on the frightening new world in which I now lived. Then each morning, I was confronted by Beth's Post-it note: 'There's no crying in rehab.' I had a job to do, and strength was required.

That job started early each morning, shortly after six o'clock. The day at HJD was organised to keep the afflicted as busy as could reasonably be expected, and designed to keep the patients' withered but motivating pride alive. An early morning shower was the perfect start to the day.

Each morning at 6a.m., the nurse who was my regular shower administrator rolled into the ward behind a hospital-issue bath chair. An Asian man of indeterminate age, his language was as blunt and severe as his haircut. He never told me his name, but in my mind I christened him 'Tenko', after the early eighties BBC drama. *Tenko* portrayed the experiences of a group of women in a Japanese internment camp during the Second World War. The women were separated from their husbands and lived in brutal conditions, facing disease, violence and death. My hot shower action was not that bad, obviously, but it didn't resemble Sean Connery being soaped up and shaved by a coven of beautiful Japanese women in *You Only Live Twice* either.

The morning after I told Beth and Joe about my Goldfinger impression, the appointed hour was approaching. I heard Tenko in the corridor, airily dismissing another nurse's plea that patient number 16 be provided with some sort of walking aid.

I imagined him hissing to his colleague behind the desk, 'He will complete his march without a chair!'

Then Tenko wandered into the ward, wheeling that bath chair. I was messed up enough to merit one, it seemed. The bath chair was not what I would have pictured: a wheeled wicker sedan for transporting a dissolute, be-dressing-gowned and syphilis-riddled member of the aristocracy. Tenko had me wrap my arm around his shoulders and eased my now skinny and saggy frame into a lightweight contraption comprised of a moulded white plastic seat attached to thin white metal legs perched on small castors. It could almost have been one of my old school's desk chairs, except for the large round hole in the middle of the seat that my newly-bony bum hung through.

Tenko had the thankless task of getting an endless roster of confused, tired and incontinent patients cleaned up first thing in the morning, and he did it with a ferocious, hilarious efficiency. In the inches between the bed and the bath chair, he inadvertently got in a fly punch to the eye and a wedgie, before he comprehensively rolled me down the hallway to the shower room.

The shower room was a large cube, the floor and walls of which were all bedecked in identical tiling. There was no boundary to indicate where the shower ended and the room began. Tenko ratcheted on the water. The running shower and the hole in which I was sitting and the diuretic pills that I was being fed each morning finally switched on that frantic feeling in my bladder. I told my commandant that I needed to urinate. He cheerily indicated I should go on the floor, and headed back into the corridor, presumably to find a heavy object that won't leave a mark when wrapped in a towel. I feared the hole in the bath chair was to allow for the *Casino Royale*-style carpet beating he was going to give my bollocks.

Yet, Tenko's morning visits became a favourite part of my day. For all my jokes about him, and his occasionally standing on my feet, he administered one hell of a shower. The only snag was, after being roused at six, I was ready for a nap when it was time for my rehabilitation classes to start around nine. Fatigue is a characteristic effect of stroke, and it's just as common after a haemorrhagic stroke like mine as it is after an ischemic stroke. Yet after I'd gratefully surrendered to Morpheus and his escape by daydream a couple of times during the day, sleep wouldn't come when the lights went off at 10p.m. I gazed at the ceiling as I lay in the prison of my broken mind, all perseveration and fear, within the darkened gaol of this strange institution.

I just wanted to go home. I tried to picture the apartment Beth and I shared, but the image wouldn't materialise. I tried to start in the bathroom, hoping I could rebuild our home from there. There must be a toilet, I thought, a sink, a bath . . . ? I could conjure nothing. Just a simulacrum of the landings on which I had delivered mail in Edinburgh during a winter twenty years earlier. Tellingly, all were anonymous, and wouldn't grant me access to the warm abodes beyond.

I was proud of the little home Beth and I had made for ourselves. The thought of getting back to it and the life we shared was what kept me upbeat. Now I realised I wasn't even sure what that goal looked like. It was a depressing thought.

On the phone that Beth had recently returned to me, I turned on some Scottish pop music to distract me from the ghostly corridors of Edinburgh tenements, and the unknown fears that stalked the hallways of HJD. Edwyn Collins's warm baritone poured into my ears again and filled my aching soul as he sang about sleeplessness and insecurity and depression.

It felt like I would never sleep again. Like I was trapped in damp rooms with no doors. Just endless, mildewed tile.

Still, I could imagine love taking me by the hand, and leading me to a bed. Our bed.

Edwyn sang about belief and renewal and getting back to the important things from the life before his haemorrhage.

As I drifted off, I thought I could feel the reassuring firmness of Beth's body materialise under my hand. Firm. Concrete. The realest thing in the world.

8

Zumba's Biggest Losers

I entered my second month of institutionalisation. I had been able to listen to music of my own choosing because Beth had begun to think that my stroke-addled brain could benefit from some gentle stimulation, and that I was just about sufficiently compos mentis to be trusted with my phone. At least within my limited and discrete personal area, I could try to remember to keep it nearby whenever I wasn't using it, under my pillow usually. Nevertheless, the first thing I would usually do whenever she arrived for a visit was ask her if she could help me find it.

'Have you looked under the sheets?'

'Yeah. I can't find it anywhere.'

'Is this it?'

Then one Sunday, she turned up with a brand-new iPad.

I think she thought I needed cheering up, after hearing each morning about my difficult nights. The day she brought in the iPad, she sat in the bedside chair and burbled away cheerily about what she had been learning about brain injuries. She had been to an aneurysm awareness group meeting at Methodist Hospital, hosted by Doctor Ayad.

'It was really interesting,' she began. 'There was this one fabulous gay guy from Ireland, and he was really funny. You wouldn't know he'd had his first hypertensive bleed in the nineties. Then he had another one more recently when he was at some out-of-town wedding.'

It turned out that after this second incident, the doctors discovered that the Irishman had suffered what he called an 'annerism'.

'Do you know what an aneurysm is, Baby?'

'It's some sort of brain thing, right?' I asked. 'But no, not really.'

I was certainly interested, though. Somebody else's woes made for a distracting diversion.

Beth told me that an aneurysm is a weak, bulging spot on the side of a blood vessel, like a thin balloon, or a weak spot on a tyre's inner tube. Apparently, around one in fifty people in the United States have one or more unruptured brain aneurysms. Including the Irishman. One of his doctors wanted to do a clipping surgery, but Doctor Ayad thought he was a candidate for coiling, instead. Coiling is a technique in which platinum wire mesh is inserted into the aneurysm, reducing or blocking the flow of blood into the little bubble. Clipping, on the other hand, describes sealing off the aneurysm with a titanium clip resembling a tiny clothes peg. The position of the aneurysm was such that Doctor Ayad was right. Now, the Irishman was recovering from his coiling, and fighting depression. He was still funny with it, though.

'He figured out he was depressed when he saw a Calvin Klein coat marked down in Macy's,' Beth told me. 'He said he even had a coupon to go with the mark-down, but he still couldn't get excited about it!'

In my cloudy state, I thought that it was just interesting and sweet that my girlfriend would be taking such an interest in neurological conditions related to brain haemorrhages. It was only months later that I realised that she had told me about this in such an entertaining manner – and had presented me with a colourful brochure from the Brain Aneurysm Foundation that explained about inner tubes and coiling and clipping – because I had been diagnosed with two aneurysms in the work-ups following my stroke.

After Beth had gone home to do the latest batch of laundry and have a glass of wine, and I had leafed through the pamphlet to pass some time, I turned my attention to the iPad, thoughtfully protected by a case in my favourite colour, red. On the back, it bore our adopted motto, an irreverent representation of the Golden Rule:

Don't be a dick.

Together, we had selected a wallpaper for the home screen. I had decided I wanted something comical and stroke-related, and we found a cartoon of an old woman helping her frustrated husband from his wheelchair to his walking frame.

'Anything you can do, I can do better,' the old woman was saying. 'I can do anything better than you.

'Do you wanna know why? 'Cause you've had a stroke, that's why!'

We thought it was hilarious.

I began to spend large amounts of time researching various aspects of my stroke and tweeting about the latest developments at HJD. When my friends responded, it cemented my presence in the outside world, as opposed to this pocket universe. If my friends could read my tweet about some whimsical thing I had learned about strokes, I must have some presence in the outside world, the real world. If I had some presence in the outside world, then I would have asserted my continuing existence. My reboot would be continuing, and I would be freed from my personal limbo.

Meanwhile, I was frequently tickled by what I would discover about my condition. In the early days after The Event – when I was still raging and insisting that when this was over, it would be time for someone else to suffer – I described myself as being 'apoplectic'. For whatever reason (too much time on my hands, probably), I realised that I wasn't quite sure why I should choose to use this word rather than just 'mad' or 'angry' or 'raging'. So I looked it up online, and was pleased to find that, as well as having the lay meaning of 'greatly excited or angered', apoplectic also means 'of, relating to, or causing stroke', or 'affected with, inclined to, or showing symptoms of stroke'.

It seemed that my mind had effected its own rehab programme. Despite the fact that I had suffered what I had incorrectly assumed was an old man's affliction, my mind was going to work out like a younger man's mind. Twitter. Wikipedia. Facebook. It wasn't time for me to lie in front of the TV with the volume blaring, waiting for the sweet release of death.

The Wee Man, however, had other ideas. So on Sunday, 4th November, the TV was blaring. Notwithstanding his ill temper and superstition, Alfonso was a Church Man who was in no shape to make it to church, so he had to have the manna of spiritual sustenance delivered by the means of television. Loud television. Television so loud that it might as well have been the voice of god – and not the still, small voice recognised by Elijah, but the voice of Metatron ringing from the heights. A voice heard in the thunder and in the roar of the sea.

My perseveration kicked in. Not the overt kind, where my brain injury would cause me to repeat a gesture or a phrase over and over and over and over again. No. The kind where my stroke-addled mind fixed onto a thought, and I couldn't shake it. I found myself unable to shake off the words of the televangelist as they sank into my ears and locked themselves into my brain. Sinful. Fallen. Gifted. Self-obsessed. Terribly uncomfortable.

While my father never expressed any interest in god or religion, my mother had been an elder in the Church of Scotland, the church of John Knox, hellfire and damnation. It was the hard, wooden pews of the Church of Scotland on which I was, to some extent, brought up, thinking of those crushes that I had told Beth about on the bench at the back of Harry Boland's.

So maybe I should have felt at home as the televangelist prattled on. But Scottish Protestantism was a hell of a lot more buttoned up than its American cousin. Maybe it was something in this difference that meant I couldn't tear my mind away. It didn't matter that the televangelist was insufferable. Nor that it sounded like his sermon was aimed at folks who already thought they were better than everyone else, especially their relatives. According to the contemporary St Paul who yelled at me through the medium of television, evangelicals' relatives were awful, with their doubt and their distrust and their disbelief, their sin and their suspicion and their scepticism. I soon learned that, even beyond that, the main problem with evangelicals' relatives was that they didn't give the evangelicals the respect they deserved. Though in my experience, people who worried about that tended to get exactly the respect they deserved.

Fortunately, the programming finally moved on. The locking jaws of perseveration weren't ready to let me go, however. St Paul's broadcast to the Apoplectics was followed by *Zumba's Biggest Losers*, an infomercial about, well, Zumba. Zumba, I learned, is a Colombian dance fitness programme. So not only were my ears being offended by a Sunday morning infomercial, they were being antagonised by an infomercial about the benefits of doing carefully choreographed steps incorporating hip-hop, soca, samba, salsa, merengue, mambo, martial arts, and some Bollywood and belly dance moves. Just to rub it in, squats and lunges were also included. Here I was, not even able to wheel myself over to the TV to carefully choreograph some martial arts through the bloody screen.

On the bright side, it soon became clear that if I could mend myself enough to dedicate my life to Christ and

Zumba, I'd soon be in great shape. Literally, as well as metaphorically.

The claims came thick and fast.

- *Zumba blends entertainment and culture into an exhilarating dance-fitness sensation!*
- *Zumba classes are fitness-parties blending upbeat world rhythms with easy-to-follow choreography for a total-body workout – that feels like a celebration.*
- *With Zumba, I lost 20lb!*
- *I'm happier, and was energised to get a new and better job!*
- *My love life is better!*
- *By following that Zumba fitness programme, I can even take over a string of Balkan and Caribbean states.*

Wait. What? Surely I didn't hear that right?

As someone on the TV was pounding away, out of my eyeshot, but sure as hell not out of earshot, the announcer informed me that our Zumba participant was feeling it in her *buttocks area*. Or *buttocks*, as a human might say. Not only was she feeling it in her buttocks, she was *smiling and sweating from start to finish* . . . Now, even I was intrigued as to what exactly Zumba might have to offer. Even if having this follow the educationally challenged version of *Thought for the Day* seemed like strange affinity marketing, at best. But soon enough, the announcer was dousing my excitement by excitedly yelling that we were 'About to meet Zumba's biggest losers!'

I rolled over in bed and tried yet again to take a nap.

9

Speech Therapy

When Tenko left me each morning, spent and abused, yet feeling tenderly cared for, the day would be ready to unfold. Our beds faced wall-mounted white boards. For the benefit of the patient and the staff, the dry erase scribblings on them were updated each day to reflect the occupant of the berth opposite, the day and date, the duty nurses and the scheduled rehabilitation activities. An early sign of progress in recovery is checking the details on the board before the doctors visit on their morning rounds.

'What year is it?'

'2012.'

'The month?'

'November.'

'What's the date?'

'Is it the seventh?'

'Yes, it's the seventh. And what day is it?'

I put on my concentrating face. 'Err . . . Wednesday?'

'Very good!'

In truth, remembering the day and date was still nigh on impossible. Cribbing off the board wasn't cheating, though. The story of the next year would be one of carefully executed coping strategies. In any event, I had to remember to look at the board, and commit all this stuff to memory for a good couple of minutes. This was good practice.

The first activity listed on the board each weekday was 'Speech Therapy'.

'I'm confused by this,' I told Beth. 'Have I been having any problems speaking?'

It turned out that a quarter, to as many as four in ten, survivors are affected by aphasia in the aftermath of their stroke. In America alone, that was one million people. The term 'aphasia' derives from the ancient Greek, *aphatos*, or 'speechlessness', though to consider it speechlessness is not quite right. Aphasia covers a whole range of language difficulties that range from losing the ability to speak, read or write, to simply having difficulty remembering words.

Our Thing was based on constant, almost pathological communication, stemming from those nights chatting on that balcony on 15th Street in the glow of another eight million people shouting, talking, whispering and murmuring like refugees from a million Martin Scorsese and Woody Allen movies. When a thought occurred to me, the first thing I would do was share it with Beth. Because it was interesting or nice, or because she could help me fashion that fragment into something useful. Or because I could share the experience of being human with someone who cared.

The problem for many people who experience aphasia is that, while their intelligence is unaffected and they can construct complicated thoughts, expression of those thoughts is difficult. Much later, Beth and I sat round a table in an Indian restaurant having a funny, interesting, emotionally and intellectually complex evening at a table populated by people coping with aphasia. During dinner, our friend Avi wanted to chip in regarding another diner's upcoming trip to Belgium. As well as being a stroke survivor, Avi worked to raise awareness of issues relating to stroke and aphasia, and ran an organisation that put together activities for disabled people in the New York area, from snowboarding to scuba diving, from rafting to rock climbing. A former emergency medical technician, he smiled easily and took pleasure from his dealings with other people. He was tracing the shape of one of those things with his finger on the cheap, white, disposable tablecloth.

You know the thing.

You know. Kind of like a grid.

You'd know it if I could show you the colour.

You eat it.

Sometimes it's made with that one thing, and sometimes it's that other stuff.

I'd tell you now, but the chatter at the other tables is distracting.

Just watch his finger. Ignore the fresh reds and greens of the kachumbar, the mango chutney, the lime pickle. Disregard the cool white of the raita.

Four horizontal lines. Then four intersecting vertical lines. Oh, what is it? It looks like that other thing . . . a grating.

I'm trying hard to grasp it, but I'm looking at the solid thought, then it turns to amorphous mush when it reaches my . . .

What's that you say? Yes, that's it! A waffle!

Afterwards, I asked Avi's friend Yvonne, who was sitting across the table from me, why it should be that the people I met who had been affected by aphasia seemed to be so nice, thoughtful, curious about their condition, and active in the stroke community.

She told me she was glad I had met so many nice, thoughtful people who dealt with aphasia. 'Remember though, that you don't hear about the many people who just stay home, depressed and despairing and angry because of their strokes.'

I noted the careful formality of her sentences.

'I would imagine that they don't, or won't, or can't, participate in life due to their strokes, especially with severe aphasia. They can't really speak for themselves! It must be hard on them.'

In contrast to my continence issues, when I asked Beth about my speech, she was able to reassure me.

'Hell, no!' she said. 'I think the nurses would appreciate it if you shut up from time to time!' She grins.

Maybe things were getting better. I may have seemed a bit batty from time to time, but since I first regained consciousness, I had been able to express whatever crazy thing had been passing through my mind without any difficulty. This was a relief. Sadly, if the symptoms of aphasia last longer than two or three months after a stroke, a complete recovery is unlikely, although with therapy, hard work and support, incremental gains are possible over a period of years, and even decades.

I got speech therapy regardless. It turned out that, notwithstanding its focus on working towards clear, organised thinking and successful expression, 'speech therapy' was a misnomer. Speech therapy covered not only speech, but also memory work, reasoning, organisation and even swallowing.

At the appointed hour, the first in what would be a string of tiny brunette speech therapists cheerily approached my bed and introduced herself as Ali.

'You know, like the boxer.' She popped stingy little jabs at imaginary butterflies floating around the bed.

She was about as much like Muhammad Ali as I was like Aly Tadros, but she knew her stuff. For a stroke patient, remembering things is about making connections that stick in the mind. A ridiculous connection can be even more effective than an apposite one.

In our early sessions, Ali would show me flashcards and ask me to identify what I was looking at. Sometimes it was clearly lettered, sans serif words. Other times, it was simple pictures of objects rendered in thick, black, cheery lines. Later, she would ask me to memorise three things.

A clock.

A truck.

A bunch of flowers.

Then, before I had to recount the items, Ali would turn over a page in the workbook that she had brought to my bedside, and read me a passage about the second president of the United States.

> Not so attentive in his studies, John Adam's favourite subject in school was mathematics. His father dearly wanted John to graduate from Harvard and become a minister. With continuous encouragement from his father and under tutelage of Joseph Marsh, John's schoolwork improved and he entered Harvard in 1751. He graduated in 1755 with Bachelor of Arts degree. Though Adams wanted to practice law after graduation, his first job was as a schoolmaster in Worcester, Massachusetts.

She closed the workbook. 'Now. Can you remember the three things, Ricky?'

'A clock. A truck. A bunch of flowers.'

I smiled. I was loving this. For whatever reason – the precise location of the lesions on my brain, the seriousness with which I was focusing on my rehab so I could get home to my partner, pure dumb luck – these tests went well. I usually finished speech therapy encouraged and energised. A competitive child of the late twentieth century, I'd had the chance to take a bunch of tests during a session and I'd passed them. Ali was an effervescent cheerleader. I was feeling good about myself.

Eventually, Ali got a new job, moved back home to the West Coast, and was replaced by another tiny brunette who didn't have a ridiculous connection to a heavyweight boxer. George Foreman, I think her name was. By this time, our activities had progressed to logic tests. I was presented with a bunch of facts, and using a grid, some connections and a process of elimination, I had to establish, for example, that George lived in the house with the green door at 3 Sandy Lane because Sophie's house had a number one lower than Jake's. That sort of thing.

'How do you think these logic problems are going to help you when you get home?' George asked one day.

My vocabulary remained healthy enough that I thought about responding, 'Are you fucking kidding me?' Something was happening in my head, though. Inappropriate behaviours were receding. I was able to self-censor, this time.

George's enthusiasm was indicative of the fact that she was a student on work experience, and she too moved on soon enough. She was replaced by Liat: the French for 'milk', but with the vowels reversed.

I made that one up on my own.

Liat was no less enthusiastic than the work experience therapist, but not quite as delusional. She and I quickly struck up a rapport. She was only slightly less tiny than the assembly line brunettes, but her smile filled a wide, rugby prop forward's face. Appropriate, because she was a South African and we shared an enthusiasm for the game. I told her about one of my childhood heroes, the international hooker, John Allan, who played for Scotland in the early nineties before returning home to play for the Springboks when they were readmitted to the fold in the wake of apartheid's abolition. Scotland and South Africa have more in common than horny-handed farmers and horny-headed front row forwards. In conversation with Liat, I recalled from my legal education that the two countries share unusual jurisprudential characteristics, in that each maintains a legal system that is founded on Roman civilian pillars supplemented by common law characteristics.

From this moment on, Liat and I were firm friends. It turned out that she had studied in Edinburgh and we both had an affection for the entertainment output of the BBC. Unusually in America, where – outside the hipster havens of

Brooklyn and elsewhere – puns truly are regarded as the lowest form of humour, we shared Alfred Hitchcock's assertion that they are the highest form of literature. I told Liat of my love of the form after she presented me with a set of quizzing puns and then each weekday, she would present me with a new set of wordplay posers. They got harder each day. Meanwhile, with the return of my phone, Beth and I had resumed our remote Scrabble games. I began rustily, but was soon playing lustily, complaining four days after the phone's restoration that the app's rejection of the proper noun *Pict* was a symbol of the oppression of my countryfolk.

Although this typically Scottish complaint was couched in Pythonesque terms – *'elp! I'm being oppressed!* – and I was doing exceptionally well in speech therapy, something inside my brain had changed. Remembering things and organising tasks took a new effort and focus. Despite – or because of – my mind's new tendency to freewheel uncontrollably, I found myself having to make an effort to slow down my thoughts and think more consciously. Without this control, my thoughts would tumble downhill. Any attempt to grasp the nearest support was a scrabbling for shallow-rooted vegetation that gave way as soon as I grabbed it, leaving me to accelerate into a car crash of jumbled, broken and dead thoughts. Something had to be done.

Fortunately, a conversation with Dawn the recreational therapist led her to come by the ward with a collection of guided meditation CDs, and I was led back to the poet Hon'ami Kōetsu's river. As my mind rebuilt itself, I had time to reflect on every thought. This was my superpower. Every thought was examined from every angle and refined before I would deem it fit for production; a tangible result that I could then sand and polish further. Eventually, it became a perfect, shiny pebble. I learned to walk it to the shore and skim it back into the sea. The stone's ripples would last for a few seconds, then it was gone.

My brain was working differently. Everyone knew this. It was time to find out why.

One cold autumn day, I was helped onto a gurney by the nurses and rolled along the corridor to the elevator bank. We took the controlled fall to the ground floor. Just as I was deciding that gurney was my new favourite form of transport, and that whoever consigned the sedan chair to history had made a serious misjudgement, the porter trundled me past the serious-looking reception desk towards the glass doors that subtly separated me from the outside world. Although I had reached a hand out to it through social media, it was still a shock to see it. As our apartment on 15th Street had receded into a bleary netherworld, there was just my ward, the therapy rooms and the office I imagined when I thought of Beth tapping away the working day. Now I knew that the outside world still existed, and it was cold.

Fortunately, our destination was right on the sidewalk: the large, silver truck that had sat quietly outside on the day I was brought to HJD contained an MRI unit.

I had never been subjected to magnetic resonance imaging before, so I wasn't sure what to expect. My father had once told me that it's a claustrophobic experience. Before I was helped onto the gurney, I had spent an hour propped up against my pillows filling in an incredibly detailed preparatory questionnaire that asked about any metal inside my body and any issues I might have with confined spaces and whether I had any cosmetic tattoos and if I had an artificial eyelid spring and if there was a bullet or shrapnel inside me. The ominous warning signs pasted to the door of the imposing silver truck were depicted in thick black lines. I didn't know what they were meant to represent, but they were not cheery, and were obliterated in turn by other foreboding, forbidding, diagonal red lines. Appropriately, my mind was quickly filled with images from comic books.

Dr Bruce Banner, bathed in the full force of mysterious gamma rays, his eyes all yellow terror and his body torn by the harsh black lines that would curse him as the Hulk.

Magneto, the nemesis of the X-Men, his face contorted by rage, unable to control his mind as it bent a metal fence.

Dr Jon Osterman bathed in radiant light, his skeleton exposed as coal-coloured daubs when he is erased from time and space. Osterman, who would painstakingly rebuild himself atom by atom and emerge as Dr Manhattan, a being with radically altered perceptions and priorities whose only remaining link to humanity was his girlfriend.

Inside the truck, I was slid onto the patient table. The patient table glided into the scanner, a grotesquely huge bobbin within which there was a magnet, gradient coils and a radio frequency coil. The inner wall of the cylinder containing me was an inch from my nose. The little jack that had been inserted into the tattered remains of my inner elbow began pushing the contrast agent into my system. The MRI technician retreated behind the cabin wall, and the process began. The machine began to buzz and clang and *Sturm und Drang*.

The noise indicated that the scanner was detecting a radio frequency signal emitted by excited hydrogen atoms in my body, using energy from an oscillating magnetic field applied at the appropriate frequency. Fun fact – in research and industry, MRI is known as NMR – nuclear magnetic resonance. The medical world prefers the term MRI.

The technician stayed behind his little wall.

My scan produced two pictures of the thought that had been niggling at my doctors. Each was longer and thinner in shape than one would imagine. Yet the magnetic images were tangible, kind of like the life described by a sonogram.

They were sclerotic-looking, like a finger in a painting by Lucien Freud, but smaller. Knobbly, like a crunchy, cheese-flavoured cornmeal snack.

But smaller.

The two terrifying brain aneurysms that cemented my transformation to this new life were each around two millimetres wide.

I knew nothing of this yet. After the scan was completed and I was wheeled back to Room 920, my unlikely miracle breezed in. She moved as easily and effortlessly as ever, as if gliding between thermals. On this day, Beth was a smiling vision, her exhaustion hidden by black ankle boots, a houndstooth skirt and caffeine molecule earrings. Unbeknownst to me, she was carefully choosing her outfit before she left the apartment each day so her appearance in the ward each morning and evening would cheer me and inspire me to come home. This didn't register with me, because she never appeared anything other than beautiful and put together in my eyes.

The effort was working, nevertheless.

Yet again, Beth took her seat next to the bed, and my claw-like left hand between hers. I could have wept with gratitude in the face of this tenderness. Of course, and as always, we had a lot to talk about. Once again, weeping would have to wait.

'How was your day, Baby?'

I told her about the interminable questionnaire and the terrible, clanging racket the machine made.

'Apparently the reason the patient information form is so long is that, if you have, say, a metal implant from before the mid-eighties inside you – or even permanent eyeliner – the machine'll pull it out of you. They're worried this will fuck you up. And their one-million-dollar machine. In ascending order of importance.

'So, to distract you from the noise, the claustrophobia and the possibility of a bullet tearing through you from the inside, you get headphones and music.'

It sounds quite calming, but I didn't get to choose the MRI playlist. If I had, I would have picked, in order of preference, not overwrought R&B vocal histrionics, not a shit Police rip-off, and not the Eagles. I had a similar take on the Eagles to Jeff Lebowski in *The Big Lebowski*: I'd been having a pretty rough time of it, and the Eagles? Let's just say, the Eagles weren't helping. Now I think about it, the source of the claustrophobia complaints seems pretty clear.

However, I'd have to imagine that no matter how much I might have appreciated it, a rehab joint couldn't get away with wall-to-wall Joy Division.

Even worse, the technician's instructions were piped straight into my brain by the headphones that were provided, too. As I lay in the capsule, surrounded by sterile white, I was quite calm. Then, over a twelve-second period, the following instructions were relayed:

'You're going to have to keep your head still.'

'Don't move your head.'

'Keep your head still.'

'Make sure you don't move your head.'

'That's it, keep your head still.'

All of a sudden, I wondered what, exactly, was going to fall out if I moved my head.

Back in Room 920, I was enjoying getting to share this human experience with someone who cared. I was transported from a world of pain and moans. Beth was in her element. Having spent weeks seven hundred miles from home during her mother's cancer treatment, she knew her way around a hospital the way a burglar can walk straight to the valuables in a strange house. She had told me before that she had been waiting for the modern world to formalise and monetise the position of 'muse'. At last, in inspiring my recovery, she had a vocational mission.

We had a fun evening together, relating our days, laughing and filling in menu cards. Then all too soon, it was time for Beth to leave.

I was tired, but as was so often the case in the evening in HJD, sleep did not come quickly. As I tortuously tossed and turned, a vision of the instrument of my transformation appeared to me. Like the Hulk's gamma rays, and Dr Manhattan's radiation, I saw my stroke constructed of angry black slashes that conveyed destruction, desolation and despair. Yet, as I turned it in my mind like a 3D model, I made friends with the angry, oval head with the matted hair, the jagged mouth and eyes like piss-holes in the snow. I decided to have his image tattooed on my left shoulder, opposite the black heart that I had had permanently inked for the temporary tattoos Beth and I had got on that early date. I had discovered I had two aneurysms, ticking like bombs in my head. It should have been a terrible day, but maybe, things were turning around.

In another part of my dream, a truck driver looked at the clock on his dashboard and accelerated, picturing the lilies he wanted to buy for his girlfriend.

A clock. A truck. A bunch of flowers.

10

Occupational Therapy and Dream States

Most mornings, the whiteboard at the end of my bed indicated that speech therapy would be followed by occupational therapy. Possibly because the very idea of OT has been derided as one step from charlatanism and quackery, occupational therapists will tell you that this branch of treatment has a long and storied history reaching back to Greco-Roman times. After falling out of favour in the medieval era, the roots of occupational therapy spread in Europe during the Enlightenment. Then, a real predecessor to OT emerged in the nineteenth century Arts and Crafts movement, which was a reaction to the monotony of work in capitalist society, even though my job in midtown Manhattan wouldn't be filled for another hundred years.

For me, OT started during my stay at Methodist Hospital. The first goal of OT is to enable the patient to master the activities of daily living, from pissing and shitting all the way to managing money. My first personal goal was to avoid bedsores, so a nurse would help me sit up in bed for five minutes from time to time. By the time I got to HJD, I was more on the 'using technology' end of the spectrum. The day after my MRI, I was escorted to a room where a computer had been set up for the patients' use. The PC sat on a plain desk, just in front of a wide, shelf-like structure that lined the window-facing wall and housed the air conditioning unit. I felt a shiver at the visual echo of my old cell on Park Avenue.

Was this why I was working so hard to recover? To be able to sub in for a young banker on the Magic Roundabout treadmill to death when he went home in the wee small hours and needed his credit facilities drafted by his lawyer?

Maybe, but I was cheered by the activity that had been prepared for me nonetheless. A kind of modified joystick had been clamped to the front edge of the desk; it was basically an unfinished block of wood. A thin, L-shaped piece of metal protruded by its foot from the front, and ended in a red, plastic gobstopper. The patient could rotate the lever around the axis of the base of the L. To have called it steampunk would have been generous. It didn't exactly look like the sort of thing you could use to pilot the Millennium Falcon through the Kessel Run in twelve parsecs.

I was instructed to manipulate a basic-looking cart through a black landscape on the screen to catch red, green, yellow and blue balloons of various sizes as they fell from the top of the screen. At the end of the session, I was promised more computer activity the next day.

When the next day arrived, Sonoko appeared to take me to that day's session. A woman of Japanese descent in her late twenties, her long, dark hair crowned a willowy frame that gave her the appearance of being taller than she was. She gained further stature from her all-business approach. That no-nonsense attitude was the reason I had decided she was not to be messed with. She was less a twenty-first century descendent of the curious Greeks than she was a modern medievalist, toting stern words instead of chains and restraints. I could understand this, given stroke's propensity for precipitating perseveration, impulsiveness and bad temper. Something of the nurses' manner with me would remind me that I was the legend who collapsed on top of his room-mate when he decided to pop to the toilet in the middle of the night despite his inability to walk, so it wasn't surprising that my OT sessions at Rusk focused on thought experiments that encouraged good decision-making and flexible thinking.

They would proceed along the following lines:

> Upon release from hospital after his stroke, Tommy is offered a job on a building site. The job involves carrying heavy loads up ladders, but Tommy is confident he can handle it. His wife is less sure. How should Tommy go about making his decision? What would you do in his position?

How to handle chip pan fires was a topic that came up with amusing regularity. One of my inspirational Post-it notes even read, 'Now you'll be really good at putting out grease fires.' I am a Scottish stroke patient, after all.

Sonoko had something fun in mind for the day's activities. 'How are you with the internet?' she asked.

A window to the outside world that's a full fourteen inches across? You've got my attention, Sonoko.

She outlined what she had in mind. 'What I want you to do is find a five-day vacation for two people. There are conditions, though. You're limited to $1,000. The vacation has to be abroad. It's got to take place in November. Also, the five days have to include a weekend. You've got an hour.'

'I'm way ahead of you, Sonoko,' I thought to myself.

This was going to be a breeze. I knew a site that handled this sort of thing. I would just plug in the variables. I knew where I was going to go, and I knew who I was going to take.

It was daydream time, and I was already standing with Beth in front of the Scottish Parliament. The abstract modernism of the parliament contrasted with the beautiful but staid Palace of Holyroodhouse across the road, which was all sixteenth and seventeenth century order standing against threats of fire, assassination and war. It was winter, and the granite of the parliament didn't glisten the way it would in the architect's Catalan home. The upturned boats of the Tower Buildings' roofs were behind us. The hulls wouldn't dry under a wet Scottish sun that hovers only an inch above the horizon. The vision stirred something in me, nonetheless. Enric Miralles's amphitheatrical parliament campus emerged smoothly from the surrounding crags, embracing tradition while striding confidently into an optimistic future. This was where I wanted to go.

This was going to be fun.

My mind was racing down the corridor as Sonoko rolled me sedately along in my chair. I was desperate to get to work. I could see the computer room and the travel website in my mind's eye, but even though we were there the previous day, I had no idea how to get there. I wouldn't even have been able to tell you about the colours of these blue corridors if I hadn't been presently passing through them. I'd been through them before, but I only existed in the moment. Unlike Miralles's magnum opus, I had no link to yesterday. Sonoko got us to the desk, though, then left me to my work.

'I'll check on you in half an hour.'

I started putting my plan into place. We could stay at the boutique hotel that looks out over North Bridge. Across from Calton Hill, where the upturned telescope of the Nelson Monument pushes into a sweeping white sky with the confidence of empire. The National Monument, Edinburgh's Folly of twelve Parthenon pillars, hiding from view beside it. In the hotel, there would be overstuffed armchairs, tartan but contemporary, to cocoon Beth and I, warm and safe as we enjoy our cocktails that taste of peat and seaweed and smoke and sex.

Sonoko arrived to interrupt my reverie. Thirty minutes had passed, and she asked how I was getting on. I was getting frustrated. I had opted for the cheapest room, and I had moved our flights along every day from Wednesday to Friday, and I was still coming in two times over budget. I would not be defeated, though. For the next thirty minutes, I scoured increasingly flea-bitten accommodations to no avail. When Sonoko deposited me back in Room 920 for a debriefing, I was able to look at the strokey scrawl of my notes and declare triumph.

'We're going to take the non-stop Continental flight to Edinburgh, and stay at my father's house!'

'You can't do that. That's cheating,' Sonoko told me.

'But I thought you wanted flexible thinking!'

I was incensed, but the unspoken rules were not to be bent. I would be allowed another attempt the next day.

For the rest of the day, I contemplated my task. This vacation hadn't even occurred to me that morning, but now it was something to look forward to, a goal. I could almost touch it. When my travelling companion arrived for her evening visit, I described my flight of fancy and its tragic end in a sea of despond.

'Did you try Canada?' Beth asked.

Oh! Canada! I should have thought of that. I once knew a wife and husband team of architects whose first major project was the interior of a boutique hotel in old Montreal. I excitedly turned to my smartphone. The hotel was easy to locate. The couple had exquisite taste, of course. Even their names sounded like they had been selected from a book of tastefully designed appellations. Their full names conjured up a few simple lines of skinny sophistication in monochrome, unfussy cladding and modern, lightweight frames. I imagined being able to sink back into my bed, swaddled by a soft and ethereal interior within the solid reassurance of a muscular Beaux Arts exterior. Or that's how the hotel's beds were described.

When I'd fantasised about visiting their early opus in another life, the architects had told me that the sushi in the immediate neighbourhood was to die for. They had lived on it for months. I would live on sashimi, Beth on California rolls. This would sustain us through days and nights of lovemaking in or around the king-sized bed. When we were sated, we would throw open the windows to a balmy, breathy breeze and enjoy our champagne cocktails looking over the roofs of Old Montreal. Or the Downtown skyline. Whichever.

When the luxury of the immaculately laundered sheets became oppressive, and the solidity of the stone, raw metal and firmly yielding bed grounded us too soundly, we would drink cheap, chilled lager with hip unknown bands in a commune in the artier part of town. This was going to be a doddle! Why hadn't I thought of it earlier?

The next day, Sonoko came back to the ward, and deposited me at the desk in the computer lab. I cracked my knuckles. Canada. I was legendary pianist Glenn Gould; Canadian, stroke-afflicted. About to create a work of art. My fingers danced across the keyboard, and with perfect synaesthesia I could taste the music in the wide stripes of chocolate, burgundy and saffron that composed the canopy of that firm bed. Then all too soon, the colours discordantly turned to ash in my mouth, and I was William Bennett, the crumpled oboist stricken on the floor of the Davis Symphony Hall. I had flown too close to the sun. I remembered entire working days at the height of my powers, contorted by the cumulative pressure of minuscule adjustments to flight schedules while looking for an affordable holiday. The room once again mutated into my old office. There was no way to get this done for $1,000. I didn't have enough time. There was never enough time.

A week later, Sonoko set me another task to train me for re-entry to the world of the living. It was the birthday of one of the physical therapists. My job, in consultation with Sonoko, was to take the number of attendees, figure out how many pizzas and bottles of soda would be required to sate them, pick out a range of toppings and flavours – allowing for dietary restrictions – call the pizzeria, and place the order, establishing the cost and time of delivery.

Despite flashbacks to my trials ordering pizzas for James Brown some seventeen years earlier in Texas, I was able to complete this task successfully. I was happy to note that there was enough veggie pizza to cover my inevitable invitation and release from the constraints of hospital food. Which turned out to be not so inevitable. Steph, the therapist who took my physical therapy the next day, said that the party went well. She admired my ordering prowess, and was just as surprised as I that this did not garner an invite.

Yet it wasn't this disregard that put me on edge around Sonoko, nor her occasionally brusque manner. On the contrary, I enjoyed her company. Not only did I admire her firm hand among the infirm, it was refreshing to be around someone who was comfortable treating me with the carelessness of adulthood. It was a change from being asked, 'Do you need to pee-pee?' As I railed against the injustices of the holiday planning task I had been set, she asked, in a casual fashion, 'Are you the kind of person who doesn't take criticism well?'

Therein lay the root of my unease. The comfort that I was slowly beginning to construct from my diminishment was the shedding of my protective dragonhide, my Mister Hyde. Yet in my rampaging, stroke patient id, Sonoko discerned the old Ricky, and tweaked him, and he didn't like it. It was he who discomfited me. I could keep him locked up in the private room where my council desk sat. Keep him hidden in the recesses of my mind, behind the door covered in red baize. Still, he would pace behind the dusty, barred windows, and mutter until his once proud voice was broken and harsh in my head. Then one day, I would think that I had need of him, and he would emerge to take away everything that I now held dear.

I couldn't allow it. My new self would have to inhabit every room, cupboard, wardrobe and door. There would be no room for that man I now found hard to describe; the one who strode upright and did not carry his strokey left arm awkwardly by his side. The man who must have been deformed somewhere, like Henry Jekyll, although I couldn't specify the exact point where or when.

As if this foggy Victorian conflict wasn't enough to postpone my sleep that night, voices of a quite tangible nature floated along the ninth-floor corridor. I couldn't tell if they came from a mob of rambunctious visitors or a bored horde of night nurses. With some difficulty, I rolled over in bed again, and fled – as I had on the night of my stroke – to the Highlands.

In a bothy in Glen Coe, an axe erupted through a red baize door, and the world of the new Ricky erupted through. There was no pea soup fog, not even a light sea haar. It was a perfect morning. The aroma of ground coffee, freshly squeezed orange juice and porridge leavened by vanilla clung to the air, competing with the chatter of stories read from newspapers bought in the village.

The wide living room was clear of chemical apparatus, crates and packing straw of the barred cabinet room. Free even from the detritus of a cosy night in front of a movie with well-buttered popcorn and generously poured whisky. The occupants of 'The Bothy' (a bothy in name only – it was well-appointed with subtle plaids and heavy tweeds) were long gone. Though not so long that the voices of their children couldn't be heard rolling down a valley that looked the same as it did three hundred years ago.

Or almost the same. If one made one's way along the base of the glen and headed up the correct hill, the wide, flat stone capping each cairn had been scraped with an 'R', a 'B', a heart and an arrow. Rural graffiti. Looking a little higher, a couple strolled by the summit, admiring the scene. Funny to think that in a few months the peak – the whole glen, in fact – would be covered in snow, and the beauty of the view would be best described as 'bleak' or 'savage'.

The man stood behind the woman, his arms wrapped around her waist. Ten years ago, her belly had been a little beach ball, swollen expectantly. He remembered this, and briefly thought of the love they had made, as they each explored her newly alien body. Now, she pinched in and curved the same way as when he was amazed by her body, as they fucked desperately in Brooklyn.

Zooming in, the love blazed from his eyes. He was still so excited to tell her about it, just like when his heart was trying to leap out of his throat that night by the jukebox at Boland's. So he moved his head a little away from hers, and bellowed into the valley:

I LOVE BETH MONAHAN!

It was clear what I had to do. The odd, subjective disturbance caused in me by Sonoko's presence was not down to anything in her. On the contrary, I was discomfited because she had no investment in my feelings or opinions, and could hold up a cheval glass, an unflinching mirror, to my unsettled gaze. I could see now that New York was my Edinburgh as much as Victorian London was Henry Jekyll's. Like Jekyll, my fondness for – the expectation that I should crave – the respect of the great and good, had led me to conceal my pleasures and carry myself in the manner expected of any upwardly mobile corporate lawyer. Just like Jekyll, when I took stock of my progress and position in the world, I found that I had been living a sort of double life – not through any malice, but a desire to fit in to the world I had inhabited. Then, for a mere thirty-three months in Beth's company, I had felt younger, lighter, happier in body, and less constrained by the bonds of obligation.

It was not that my new self was in any way base or dangerous. My former, be-suited, Midtown self may have recused himself from taking any part in the financing of an arms manufacturer, but he was still a minuscule cog in the machine that had brought the world economy to its knees. The bearded, tattooed two-and-a-half-year-old who had embarked on the process of blundering out of that life when he met Beth Monahan was a harm to no one. Not even himself, night-time stumbles aside.

I thought he deserved a chance to make something of himself. That wasn't going to happen in New York, however, where too many people would expect more of the same, where every shadow would conceal a silent disapproval of my betrayal of the kid in that dark, stony basement of the Old College.

'Beth and I will make a new start in Scotland,' I thought to myself. I could already see the heather-clad moors in my mind's eye.

But I still had no idea how to get there.

11

Physical Therapy

Stroke brings out the best in us. Stroke brings out the worst in us.

A fellow survivor once told me he lives in fear of his own fathomless fury.

'I had been doing my grocery shopping. I was really frustrated. There was music playing in the store. It was hard to concentrate, and make out what people were saying. I was trying to lift a package of soda bottles off the shelf, and it kept catching on the package underneath. This guy behind me – he wanted soda too – got impatient. He said to me, "Why don't you use both hands?!" I shook my useless right side at him, and then stormed out without finishing my shopping. Outside, I started to cross the road. I was using my stick.'

He put the walking stick on the table for emphasis. It was wrapped in different coloured tapes, the least festive candy cane you can imagine.

'Do you know why it's red and white?' he continued. 'It's so people can see I have trouble with my vision and hearing. Then this other guy, he just zooms up, before slamming on his brakes at the last second. I was furious. I waved my stick and slammed it down on the hood of his car. Then he got out. He was very big, and very angry. But look at me. I couldn't fight. I couldn't flee.'

'Then what happened?'

'I think he took pity on me.'

In the face of too much pity and sympathy – 'Oh god, it must be terrible!' – some stroke survivors become obsessed with empathy.

Joyce Hoffman, a stroke blogger of my acquaintance, described her experience: 'Only a couple of people in my life empathised with me. Fellow stroke survivors can automatically empathise because they know the absolute hell that I've been through. Other people seem to find it a lot more difficult.'

Brené Brown, a research professor at the University of Houston Graduate College of Social Work, gave a talk about empathy a couple of years before my brain exploded. She noted that, while empathy fuels connection, sympathy drives disconnection. She made the point that, when things are at their worst, sometimes making a connection is more important than trying to come up with what feels like the right response.

Stroke was the great democratiser. The great leveller. It imposed empathetic imagination.

At the beginning of November, I was standing at the door of the gym at HJD, where those of us who could make it out of bed would do our physical therapy. The wall beside the door, as well as the wall at the far end of the room, was lined with the mats where each individual's therapy session would start. Our therapists called them 'mats', but they were so different to the mats you see in a proper, gym-type gym, that this would just drive home our otherness.

The mats were a quiet blue, of course. Almost everything in HJD was blue. I was drowning in blue. Blue tones are associated with feelings of relaxation – the city of Glasgow once put up blue street lighting, and it was said to reduce crime. In Nara, Japan, prefectural police set up blue street-lights and they reported that crime fell. In Yokohama, a railway company installed blue lights at the ends of their platforms to try to reduce suicide.

101

In the gym, the blue, waterproofed cloth material of each mat covered a padded platform, about five feet by seven, within a metal frame. The platforms appeared to hover about eighteen inches off the ground, each supported by an inconspicuous galvanised metal framework that was mostly hidden by the platform. The car crash outlines of the patients' bodies were arranged on these platforms as their therapists manipulated atrophied limbs as a warm up.

Unusual as the mats were, it was the patients who brought my scattered attention into focus. I looked over by the parallel bars and thought they must be for aiding the first, faltering crack at walking – I didn't think I could manage the dismount if they required something more ambitious. Next to the apparatus, there was an elderly husband helping his wife through rehab, and learning techniques to help her after discharge. Watching them, I thought it was the most romantic thing I'd ever seen.

Otherwise, the scene was a shocking parade of tattooed-up under-forties with hipster haircuts and glasses. I had told Beth, who had written a dating and relationships advice column for her business school newspaper, that there was an article in directing New York's young, single men and women to the stroke wards. The gym was full of skinny, funny, well-accessorised young men with cool tattoos and, more lucratively, older, more fragile men, too. Remembering the 35lb I had lost, I could understand why they were skinny. I got why they were funny. Over the next year, we would meet a host of supporters and carers who would describe how the thing that got them through the darkness of stroke was their loved one's hilariousness. I subsequently discovered that a bleed in the frontal lobe has been found to reduce inhibitions, so survivors often have no filter and say the most outrageous things.

It took me a long time to come up with a theory on the prevalence of the skin ink. I had two tattoos at the time, too.

One was the black heart on my right shoulder. It was a perfect replica (but 25 per cent bigger – to scale) of the one on Beth's left shoulder. It was my first tat, at the age of thirty-five. Beth's too, at thirty. About the right age for that sort of thing, I think. Beth would proudly show off her newly adorned skin and receive glowing compliments. Then I'd unveil mine to a chorus of clicking and tutting, as the realisation of the reality of the matching tattoo sank in with the observers.

On the left shoulder, a complicated latticework of circles and lines representing *Doctor Who*'s Time Lord Seal decorated my skin. This was a birthday present from Beth. It was meant to represent the infinite possibilities of life. All of the potential adventures in time and space. It was also a reminder that there's strength to be found in the least expected places, even when things are at their bleakest.

I remember sitting at home as a wee boy, watching *Doctor Who* with my mum and dad. I remember being scared by a man who pulled off his human face to reveal a pesto-coloured mess of tendrils. Laughing at the antics of Tom Baker and his patrician yet anarchic portrayal of the ancient man who valued the child within, I'd scoot onto my father's armchair and enjoy being scared by robots and cyborgs and aliens. Practicing for real fear and death, untouchable on a Saturday evening.

Now, my story incorporated a companion who knew what I needed, even before I did. Someone to travel with me who made me better. Just like the companions who travelled with my fictional hero.

When the tattoo was finished, Beth asked the inker if he was happy with it.

He told us he was. 'Other tattoo artists will really appreciate this,' he said. 'Circles and fine lines are difficult. It's cruel to have your tattooist work on this first thing on a Saturday morning.'

It was 2p.m.

I finally concluded that the gym was awash with the patients' ink because tattoos are – still, just about – a signifier of recklessness, rebellion and abandon. Haemorrhagic strokes remain popular among the relatively young despite intensive efforts to reduce the prevalence of risk factors such as smoking, hypertension and alcohol abuse. Medical professionals speculate that this may be due to a lack of impact of risk factor reduction measures among younger people and reckless rebels who wear their sleeves on their arms.

It wasn't only the patients in the gym who were young. The physical therapists were young, too. Just like all of my therapists. Just as my father knew he was getting old when all the policemen started looking young, all my therapists were some undefined age that was best described as 'younger than me'. As I stood at the threshold of the gym, a strobe light of insight flickered into life. Maybe I would never stand inside a cube of sweating whitewashed walls again, my hands to the ceiling, my eyes to the light, happily being jostled by fellow revellers. Maybe I wouldn't ever dance again.

Did the kids even rave in dank, under-the-stairs clubs anymore?

Throughout my stroke experience, the physical therapists were my favourite therapists and they had the best equipment, too. Towards the beginning of my time at HJD, Michelle, my weekday PT, got together with her colleague, Rodney, and helped me arrange myself on the obviously blue floor of the gym. The two therapists were compact little balls of health who worked with an efficiency that suggested they could take care of me as successfully as they had taken care of themselves.

Michelle relieved me of my left trainer and stuck a mark of infirmity on the inside sole of the shoe, under the heel. It was about the size and shape of a hen's egg, perfectly matching the olive-grey of the shoe's outside wall. Without prior knowledge of my situation, you wouldn't have known that it wasn't part of the original design. The egg quietly pressed into my foot like the black spot blind Pew pressed into the hand of Billy Bones, summoning him to his death by thundering apoplexy. Meanwhile, Rodney wrapped a lightweight grey and blue cuff around my leg, just below the knee. The cuff had a plastic casing set in one side that held a device resembling a pager. When Michelle had finished applying the conductive fabric sticker, she attached the gait sensor to the trainer, while her colleague began to program the remote control.

All these items worked together as what the manufacturer, Bioness, called the L300 Drop Foot System. The system delivered small electrical stimulations in a timed pattern set by the remote control. The idea was that those impulses would activate the muscles in the leg to lift my foot to take a step. Except I was not ready to take independent steps. Even walking with foot drop was a dream. Instead, while I lay on the ground, my rehabbers lashed my reshod feet to a stationary bike. With the help of the artificially created impulses, I was able to cycle in a pleasing, mechanical rhythm. My inner sci-fi geek was elated! Lying on the floor, I pictured myself rampaging through Tribeca on Inspector Gadget-style mechanical legs. Or relentlessly marching up the East Side after having all my organic parts replaced so that, incrementally, I became a cyborg. Or sprinting uncontrollably north along Second Avenue, while Rodney and Michelle cacklingly controlled my limbs.

A week later, Michelle guided me to a small room – a large cupboard, really – and introduced me to the Bioness Dynavision D2. It was a black, four-foot square board, dotted with a constellation of little, square, red and green LEDs that radiated from its centre. While I stood on an instability pad, individual LEDs blinked randomly. If a green LED flashed, I was to press the button it illuminated. If it was red, I was to control my impulse. In either event, I had to recite the number that appeared on the board, at eye level. It was like *Dance Dance Revolution* for stroke patients, and it was intended to help with visual, motion and attention deficits for patients with neurological injuries. I loved it.

When we returned to the main gym room after that activity, my crackling peripheral vision picked out the poster on the wall furthest from the door, and I focused on it. Big, happy letters like you might see on a primary school project told me I was looking at a collection of photos of those who have passed through rehab in this gym before, and had entered THE NEURO-REHAB HALL OF FAME. In each picture, an all-star stood, grinning, among a row of triumphant therapists.

'How do I get up there?' I asked Michelle.

'Just keep working.'

I told her that making it onto the wall was my new ambition.

Physical therapy became the tent pole that supported my entire rehabilitation. While my brain found it hard to gauge its own improvements, the gains PT produced were measurable, tangible and of huge encouragement. The elation these gains brought would radiate, like an exploding pattern of green and red lights, to improve my performance in speech therapy and occupational therapy.

I woke up on 3rd November and tweeted: '*Yay! Saturday! Even inpatients deserve a weekend.*'

Generally, there was no speech therapy during the weekend, and I was free of occupational therapy, too. On this day, my excitement arose because Steph, my weekend physical therapist, had noted my enthusiasm and asked if I would like double sessions at the weekend. I leapt at the chance. I loved physical therapy, and weekends in HJD had a tendency to drag. Beth would make her regular visits on the weekend – more, even – but with the paucity of therapy sessions, there was still too much time to fill.

It didn't hurt that Steph also seemed to enjoy our therapy sessions. We were good company for each other. After my catastrophic stroke, my relative youth still allowed room for important gains, and I displayed a cheery enthusiasm for PT. Steph responded well to the irreverence I have osmosed from Beth. She was tickled by my apparent invention of the word 'rehabber', and enjoyed my imaginary dismount from the parallel bars. This seemed appropriate. In contrast to Sonoko's unremarkable prettiness, Steph's handsomeness was quirkily notable, like that of a comedienne who unfurls her hair to gasps in the final act. It wasn't so much that she was beautiful, more that her laugh and that smile had warmed the audience to her over the period of the feature. The smile that dominated all of her other features denoted a certain *joie de vivre* that complemented her devotion to her vocation. I liked to think that she would have been a lot of fun over a couple of pints in Boland's.

On this particular Saturday, Steph arrived to take me to the gym. When we got there, she watched me go through a series of exercises. I dragged myself up the four steps of the wooden staircase in the corner. They were stairs to nowhere, ripped out of the context of a home or a place of work. My left side had always been so dominant that, when playing football, I'd personified the barb, 'His right leg's for standing on.' Now, both legs simply provided straightened, straitened support while my arms did most of the work supporting me, and I progressed along the parallel bars. Then Steph walked me through the basics of using a walking stick.

The hospital had issued me with a cane that was a beautifully ergonomic piece of kit, nothing like the hook-handled, straight, wooden canes the old women in my mother's church had used. It ran black from its foam handle through the crook that let me drive my weight through my forearm, down its metal body to the triangular rubber foot that allowed it to stand alone, unsupported.

If you've ever walked with a walking stick, you'll know it takes a bit of learning. Firstly, you hold the cane in the hand that's on the good side. Initially, I found this counterintuitive; it was the weak side that needed the support, surely? Thankfully not, since my left arm was as useless as my left leg for now. Think about how you walk. If you're able-bodied and you're walking, you swing your arms as you walk. When you take a stride forward with one foot, the opposite arm swings forward.

Holding the walking stick in my right hand allowed my right arm to absorb some of my weight as I walked. I was like Jake the Peg in that old song my mother sang to me as a child, with my extra leg. I followed a straight line down the centre of the gym, treadmills and apparatus forming an honour guard. My good middle foot moved forward and touched down, followed by my two side feet, the left and the little rubber triangle.

It was as complicated as it sounds. It turned out that, even for the able-bodied, walking is a little miracle of perfectly timed moments. Most of the time, we don't think about it. Even toddlers are expected to do it without a detailed breakdown of the constitutive elements. What I discovered was that walking is like a golf swing – with thousands of hours of practice, it simply becomes second nature, a matter of muscle memory which propels us effortlessly down the fairway. When we're not expert, and have to think about each of the steps, things fall apart. The recovery of my weakened left knee was imperilled by a tendency to hyperextend, snapping my limb violently in and out of a straight-legged attention. I had to focus on walking heel-to-toe, a broken ceilidh dancer, so my left foot wouldn't flatly slap on the floor like a lemon sole on an Edinburgh fishmonger's counter. Even swinging my arms in an opposite pattern to my legs required thought, as I had a tendency to carry what Beth would call my stroke-afflicted *T. rex* arm curled in halfway up my torso.

Watching me turn to begin another short length of the gym with my stick, Steph pointed out another aberrant movement. As I turned, my foot didn't swivel around the axis of my ankle; I had to move my whole leg. The movement was unnatural, and multiplied my turning circle. After being made aware of the shortcoming, I still couldn't complete the manoeuvre. Watching Steph demonstrate how one's foot turns a corner, I tried to copy the action. My attempts improved in increments, before sliding back as I tired. There wasn't a bit of kit to help with this, but Steph had an idea. We sat together to form an islet in the sea of blue floor as she took off her right sneaker.

'Give me your left,' she instructed.

My newly inexpert fingers fumbled the laces, and I wrenched the left shoe off my unfeeling foot. Steph produced a roll of what looked like black electrical tape from nowhere, about half-an-inch wide, and gaffa-ed our shoes together.

'OK,' she declared, pleased with her impromptu handiwork. 'Put your shoe on, then I'll slip into the other side, and we'll practice.'

That's what we did. First, we stood together. Without having to think, Steph helped support me and curled her right foot through a short, easy curve. My left foot could only follow, but quickly, the movement began to feel natural. Even graceful, by my monstrous standards. Of course, that was the idea. With the brain lesions, and the atrophy, and the nerve damage running down my left side, I had no memory, and no muscle memory, of the movement. We were rebuilding it from scratch. Soon enough, something triggered. We sat on the edge of a mat and Steph extracted her foot from her invention. I followed suit, and she cut our shoes apart with a pair of short-bladed, ring-handled, surgical scissors. Where the hell were all these supplies materialising from? My trainer was restored to me, and I repeated the move, just me and my extra leg. Another breakthrough!

A few days later, on 9th November, Michelle came to pick me up for another PT session. Earlier, a nurse had helped me locate the latest fresh set of workout clothes Beth had washed and brought from 15th Street. I dressed myself according to the instructions Sonoko had provided in occupational therapy. I sat on the edge of the bed, under a nurse's supervision. I used my strong arm to dress my weak side first, for each piece of clothing. After I had complained about the cold up here on the ninth floor, Beth had brought me a pair of long, black, thermal underwear made by a sportswear company, over which I managed to put on a pair of grey shorts that almost reached my knees. A similarly sporty T-shirt in a cotton and polyester blend was covered by another, long-sleeved, cotton T-shirt in a lighter shade of grey. It had been a good morning, and I was amused by the reflection of my skinny frame's covering of baggy T-shirt and, basically, black tights. I looked like a particularly unwell example of an early nineties grebo-punk. I tweeted my amusement to my friends: '*Showered, dressed, breakfasted, Beth Monahan'ed. A good morning. If one can overlook that I'm dressed like a member of Ned's Atomic Dustbin.*'

The response came quickly. Going by the time stamp, Beth must have been on her way to work. '*Hey! I picked those clothes out!*'

I clarified that it wasn't an insult. I was discovering a newly scraggy body with a lack of inhibitions and an almost total absence of judgement. If my broken brain was going to dress me as a nineties British pop star, I'd have been checking if I could now pull off Brett Anderson's half-unbuttoned, body-painted acrylic blouse. So things could have been worse. Fortunately, Michelle was spared that indignity as she escorted me along the square corridor that ran around the ninth floor. In light of recent advances, I was walking with only the support of the flat, ridged plastic handrail that sidled around the walls. Concentrating on the minutiae of the components of walking, I didn't see a troop of rehabbers passing.

'Ha! You look ridiculous, Ricky!'

We hadn't advanced to looking around while shambling, so I stopped and checked my hold on the handrail before looking around. I wasn't a person to whom people called out. I was just a shambly stroke patient.

But Steph had. That comedienne's laugh reached along the walls.

It was when my therapist heckled me that I knew I was out of the woods.

12

The Magic Rutabaga

It was after not being allowed solid foods, and then being appalled by puréed bread and most of the other soft slop that had been served to me at mealtimes, that I had lost that 35lb.

Back when I was at Methodist, one of the doctors had taken Beth aside in the corridor.

'Go and find something he likes,' he had said. 'It doesn't matter what it is. As long as he eats something.'

'He does enjoy those chocolate and vanilla puddings that sometimes come with his dinner.'

'Perfect. Go down to the cafeteria, and get a bunch of them.'

We took this direction seriously. Supplies from the cafeteria supplemented the lunchtime and dinnertime nutritional puddings I was already being served, and to the extent I couldn't finish them, they were hoarded in the bedside cabinet for later. Now, Beth would also pop into the Barnes & Noble bookstore on her way to HJD, to pick up a cup of tea for herself, and a cream puff for me. The cream puffs tasted like they had been baked in small batches by a Brooklyn fairy godmother from flour, butter, eggs, salt and heavy cream, and then covered in smooth, intense chocolate.

However, a Scotsman with a stroke cannot live on cream puffs and puddings alone. As my activities in therapy stepped up, Beth would sit by my beside each evening, ticking boxes on a menu as I declared my preferences for the next day's meals. She did this partly to be, and feel, helpful, and partly because she was concerned I would forget that I'm a vegetarian, only to remember with horror when I realised what I had been eating.

One night, I opted for an impossibly exotic side dish. Dinner arrived the following evening, and I tucked in.

'What is this stuff?' I asked.

Its appearance offered no clue, so Beth took a tentative taste. 'That's your pureed rutabaga,' she declared.

'Oh! So *that's* pureed rutabaga? I don't like it.'

I didn't like the taste of it at all, but I loved the word 'rutabaga'. A rutabaga may look like a neep on steroids, but I subsequently learned that it's a cross between a turnip and cabbage, with all the exciting flavour explosions that would suggest. Still, the word took root in the surprisingly fertile soil of my re-wiring brain. An 'eggplant' may not hold a candle to the romance of the 'aubergine', but a 'rutabaga' suggested heights of exoticism that a 'swede' could not touch.

By the end of the day, I had sketched my imaginary new friend, The Magic Rutabaga, on a napkin. Tottering on wispy legs, two thick leaves parted above his giant head, and he looked bloody furious. His eyes squeezed shut in disgust at the gods who had condemned him to bland flavourlessness, his uvula swung as he yelled, 'AAARGH!'

Our pal Paul took a look at the tortured countenance of Rudy the Magic Rutabaga and noted, 'Once a year, in early February, he rises from the basement and feels bad about not being The Great Pumpkin.'

'Great for scaring kids, though,' I told him. ' "If you don't eat yer veg, The Magic Rutabaga's gonnae get ye." Even I'm scared.'

'You could make it a Valentine's Day special. *The Magic Rutabaga Falls in Love*. His mom is mad because his girlfriend's kale.'

'Yeah, but The Magic Rutabaga is all about tolerance and acceptance and good nutritional values.'

Paul had a six-year-old daughter, and knew that kids are predisposed to the triumph of good and ridiculousness. 'That's it!' he declared. 'We're writing a children's book!'

Meanwhile, he and Beth were doing their bit to brighten up my nutritional regime. Beth had brought me a canister of fancy tea bags to replace the brackish horror of water contamination that was the hospital tea. It had a ridiculous name that was only made more absurd by the appending of its self-applied sobriquet, 'The Aristocrat of Teas'. Everything about the replacement Beth brought was better. These new bags were encased in a properly upscale, hexagonal red tin. Its lid fitted with a satisfied expulsion of air. The smooth silkiness of the bags themselves shone with a heavenly glow. I quite liked them, and declared as much to Beth when she arrived for her morning visit.

'I'm finding that the hospital breakfast is immeasurably improved by that Barney and Sons Royal English Breakfast Tea.'

'What . . . ? Oh, it's not Barney, Honey. It's *Harney*.'

'Och. Those posh English and their made-up names. Tell Harney I'm sorry. And tell the boys, Hernard and Hartholomew, too.'

Paul's contribution rounded out breakfast nicely. He had asked Beth round for family breakfast on the morning of Sunday, 4th November. His apartment, tastefully and functionally appointed in the modern fashion of a well-to-do man who knows the value of things, smelled of baking bread. As befits a man with a PhD in black hole physics – and I have a theory that while cooking is an art, baking is a science – the flat more precisely smelled of flour, butter, salt and yeast that had interacted at exactly the right times and at the right temperatures to create a satisfyingly chewy, bready bread. The source of the scent sat in the kitchen, wrapped in an appropriately traditional dishtowel, with a knife nestled in the turned-over material.

Beth dutifully delivered the delightful little bundle to my ward. The blessed package was a testament to the paucity of the English language. It would be an insult to Paul to let this beast of the yeast go by the same name as the soggy square that had previously besmirched my plate. This was *manna*.

In fact, it went by a number of names. Paul had trailed its arrival as following 'The Great Home Loaf Delay Experiment'. I guessed that this had something to do with his scientific method, but still harboured a suspicion that he was discussing some obscure prog rock band I hadn't heard of before. Knowing that while spinning in the void, I was using my phone as a tether to the mothership of my old life, Beth and Paul co-ordinated the picking up of the bread through their Twitter accounts.

'*This just in*,' Paul tweeted. '*Ricky's loaf! (See you around 10.30, Beth.)*'

My nurses were rather less excited. After the loaf had arrived, Maria eyed my table suspiciously.

'You're not allowed to have that,' she said, confiscating the butter knife and its six-year-old-appropriate serrations.

'But . . . it's not mine. It's a friend's. He made me the loaf. I can't let you have his knife!' Notwithstanding my apoplexy and my lack of inhibitions, I was too shocked and institutionalised to complain properly.

'I'll give it back to Beth when she comes.'

'Is it a safety issue? What do you think I'm going to do with it? Hijack the hospital? I don't even know where the cockpit is!'

My pleas fell on deaf ears. Later in the day, Beth got the knife back and returned it to me.

'Be discreet with it,' she whispered, so when not in use the knife was tucked away in the folds of the dishtowel.

As was only right, my safety was the paramount concern of the hospital staff. One weekend in the aftermath of Hurricane Sandy, the kitchen was closed, and the nurses relayed our lunch orders to the amusingly named deli down the road. *Divine!* With an exclamation mark! Excited to get some proper food from the outside, I ordered the veggie burger. It was *Average! At best!* Still, it was better than the grilled cheese sandwich, which was *Decidedly Ropey!*

Worse was to come. Each evening, when Beth and I meticulously checked and ticked my next day's meal plan, we were looking for stuff I would eagerly gobble, especially protein. Each day, more slop arrived. My only salvation was breakfast, consisting of a single-serve box of Special K, a thick slice of Ricky's Loaf, slathered with jam and salty butter, and a cup of hot, posh tea.

'*Posh tea*,' I tweeted. '*Thanks, Beth! Also, suck it, plebs!*'

Impulse control was still an issue, though not all the time. Every evening when we weren't ordering from the deli, I would take my little pencil and cross out the qualifier 'soft' on all my menu options, and circle the word, 'sautéed'.

I remarked to Beth, 'It seems less confrontational than scrawling "I didn't break my jaw!!!" on the menu in my own blood. Also, three exclamation marks would be half an armful.'

It was a shame that my pleas were to no effect. When their food wasn't watered down and pureed, the kitchen at HJD did some great work. One day in mid-November, for example, I was served thyme-roasted zucchini sticks. They smelled dubious, but I was delighted to find they tasted of zucchini. Thyme, too! So I pleaded some more with my nurses and doctors to let me eat at the grown-ups' table.

When Liat arrived in the morning to chat rugby and other matters over word games, I related my woes. 'What they told me is, the kitchen's records have been left in disarray by the hurricane. Since we're all presumptive choke risks, they're having to be conservative, and everyone on the floor is getting soft food. Speech therapy has to approve my request.'

'Your vocabulary's not really been affected, has it?' Liat remarked.

Each morning, Liat wold assure me that the kitchen had been informed of my chewing and swallowing skills. Each day, nothing would change.

Nevertheless, other improvements in my condition were becoming evident. My reckless impulses were being curtailed by occupational therapy. It seemed Sonoko was still concerned about grease fires, and every few days, I was asked again how I would handle one. I wondered if this had anything to do with the adventurous attitude Americans display around cooking oil. Every Thanksgiving, apocalyptic videos of turkeys deep frying flood the Internet. Burning barrels of bubbling, boiling oil. Trees being exfoliated as fat leaps into the air. Children running, their anguished faces framed by fire. Burning oil clinging to homes like sticky napalm.

Then I thought again, and decided this had everything to do with my Scottish accent. We Scots will deep-fry anything. Twenty-three years had passed since the first time I ate deep-fried pizza from a chippy, and twenty-three years later, I could still taste the three-day old chip fat the pizza had absorbed until it was bloated to a multiple of its regular size. Maybe this was why I had resisted the temptation of the deep-fried Mars Bar for so long.

Beth tells me I have to be careful with the terminology here. So, for our American friends:

- *Your Mars Bars are our Topics.*
- *Your 3 Musketeers are our Milky Ways.*
- *Your Milky Ways are our Mars Bars, which are yummy when battered, deep-fried and sprinkled with powdered sugar.*

- *Don't get me started on renaming Marathons as Snickers. I'm still furious.*

The unusual abstemiousness I had displayed in avoiding the deep-fried Mars Bar could have been ascribed to their being for tourists. Something an Edinburgh Festival-time visitor would breathlessly inhale as his nylon-clad arms, akimbo but *zwip-zwipping* against the fluorescent plumage of his torso, attempted to propel him along Edinburgh's Royal Mile. There was no need for shame in Park Slope, however, where The Chip Shop on Fifth Avenue marketed the deep-fried Mars Bar as ironic exoticism.

Although Sonoko would narrow a nostril and purse a lip at me attempting to operate a deep-fat fryer, a barbecue was an American Dream to which I was allowed to aspire.

'Today, I want you to plan a barbecue for friends,' she told me at my next occupational therapy session. 'Where are you going to host it?'

'How many people are you going to invite?'

'What are you going to make?'

'What will you need to buy?'

'What's everyone going to drink?'

'What about dessert?'

As usual, I partially flunked my occupational therapy test. I thought I could fashion a pretty good meal out of non-animal produce. Garlic bread. Corn. Aubergines. OK, 'eggplant'. Yes, eggplant parmesan. Some veggie hot dogs. We would need buns and mustard and ketchup. This plan and its apparent contempt for my guests was batted away as yet another symptom of my inflexibility, so I offered up some halibut or salmon to assuage any blood lust on the part of the imagined mob. This latest sign of progress was enough for me to be awarded with an attempt at cooking for real. For the next day, I had to pick out something cheap and easy to make in a microwave. Sonoko would get hold of the ingredients, and I would make it the day after that.

'If you want to eat well in England,' W. Somerset Maugham once opined, 'you should have breakfast three times a day.' I decided to knock up some scrambled eggs. Two days later, Sonoko came to Room 920 and escorted me to the patients' kitchen. Unlike the cramped scullery of any apartment I had lived in in New York City, it was a capacious cookhouse, with room to whirl a wheelchair, never mind swing a cat.

Across the plains of the work surface, Sonoko arranged the supplies I had requested expansively, but within reach. A watery winter sun poured through the windows that ran along the wall of the canteen, and splashed across the eggs, butter, salt and pepper, and milk. A fork and a knife of appropriate bluntness sat in readiness next to a small Pyrex jug.

Sonoko and I had discussed the steps I would take to conjure a fluffy scramble on our way to this orderly mess room. Now practiced in the use of a walker in my physical therapy, I propped myself against the counter and begin to methodically follow those steps, outlining each step as I was about to embark upon it. Sonoko offered little bits of guidance, or asked questions to prompt adjustments, as if I was her grandmother and she was teaching me how to suck the eggs. This was good, because beginning to take small steps, like preparing a simple meal, was nerve-wracking even though it was a process I had completed countless times before.

Beth had a theory similar to Maugham's: if you want to have a man make a good meal, have him prepare breakfast. After our first night together, I had slipped quietly out of bed, leaving her to sleep, and parachuted down to the coffee shop on the corner. I brought back two coffees, one latte and one flat black, neither sugared, both accompanied by various types of sweetener. This modular presentation, convertible into any one of a number of hot libations, was intended as an indication of capability. Of mindfulness. Innumerable weekend breakfasts would follow, during which I would learn how to accommodate our different tastes in eggs – her, either finely scrambled or fried with the yolk broken, always well done; me, over easy or comprised of thick and soft, lightly turned curds.

Production of this meal was a guided meditation, Sonoko's instructions returning my focus to the immediate action whenever my mind strayed or ran ahead. Still, hobbling from thought to thought and trying not to slip between the gaps, my mind dilated time. The yolk of the first egg slithered into the jug, and I thought of Beth's dislike of a soft yolk. I thought of Paul and his wife, Jen, and their small family farm in Pennsylvania. I thought of what they had told me about the benefits of a poultry saddle.

A poultry saddle looks just like its equine equivalent, and I love the idea of a little Beatrix Potter anthropomorph zig-zagging among the apple trees on a speeding hen. However, the function of a poultry saddle is to protect the hen from feather-scalping, rooster spurs and even death, at the hands of a very large cockerel. An industrial farm is unlikely to fund poultry saddles, even for a useful piece of capital like a brood hen, so the hens are kept in single-sex facilities.

Beep. Beep. Beep. Beep. Beep. Beep.

The microwave brought my attention back to the task at hand. I pressed the button and the microwave door popped open. My damaged dominant hand shook as I slowly, ever so slowly, removed the steaming jug from the thick glass turntable. I held the jug handle in that hand, so my previously neglected, impotent right could fluff the mixture.

The eggs came out well. A sprinkling of grated cheese added a pleasing texture. I was discovering that little things were to be enjoyed more than ever. I was still alive after almost being not alive.

What did that mean, though? Since the time of the ancient Greeks, we've had a terrible time expressing exactly what differentiates life from what is not alive. Soon enough, this stroke patient would read Ferris Jabr write in *Scientific American* of how the standard biology textbooks that define life have been reduced to replicating shopping lists of distinguishing characteristics. There are always exceptions, however. Crystals are highly organised and grow. Fire consumes energy and gets bigger. Some crustaceans can enter long periods of dormancy during which they are not growing, metabolising or changing at all. And on and on.

In planning the ongoing search for life, an advisory panel to NASA came up with what they hoped was a lucid, concise and comprehensive definition of life: a self-sustaining system capable of Darwinian evolution. This doesn't work either. According to this definition, a parasitic worm living inside a person's intestines isn't alive. Certain modern computer programs and platforms, on the other hand, do evolve and mutate within a self-contained context. RNA enzymes – or ribozymes – also satisfy the test. A member of the NASA advisory panel suggested that ribozymes mean we have to add another element to the test: to be alive, an organism needs to be *inventive, needs to come up with new solutions*. Already, we're heading back to the textbook shopping list.

Jabr concluded that the reason we can't come up with a specific set of physical properties that clearly separates the living from the inanimate was because no such thing exists. To put it another way, there's no such thing as 'life'. It isn't a thing. It's an adjective. It describes a level of complexity. A level of complexity such that its shutdown will make us cry. An operation of zeroes and ones sufficient to make the gods weep thunderstorms of pathetic fallacy.

As I lay in bed that afternoon, the sun shone through the window of Room 920 and I generated a cosy warmth under the hospital-cornered bedclothes. It was the warmth of the atoms within the egg molecules being reorganised and releasing energy. Twenty per cent of that energy would be used for brain metabolism. My complex machine still worked, in a fashion, after its power indicator had flickered off. Its operations were still a bit unpredictable, sure, but maybe that could be fixed. I needed to decide to be alive – to be inventive, come up with new solutions.

I tapped at the iPad. The list of things I would have to do when I resumed Life was growing.

'Consider veganism,' I wrote.

I opened another note, and wrote to the slim vegan with the toned musculature who didn't exist. Yet.

'I must never accept defeat. I must succeed. I must come back stronger.'

There is no such thing as life, yet it can blink out in an instant.

13

Quiet: Patients are Healing

Now my memory works in a way that approximates that of a real boy, I pretend to myself that I can remember more detail of the autumn of my stroke than I really can. It was a momentous time – for better or worse, nothing would be the same again.

I do, however, retain a sensation of the terror that the nights would bring when the nurses would withdraw to chatter at their stations and the only figures by my bed were the vivid regrets of years past and the dark, long-fingered threats of the future reaching back into the present. That's why, one night in early November after I had begun to show the first guttering flickers of rational thought and Beth had returned my phone, I tried in my mind to reconstruct the reassuring little apartment we shared.

It was impossibly ambitious. I couldn't remember what the apartment looked like at all. Once again, I recalled a detail of the bathroom and tried to rebuild from there, conjuring a dinosaur from a thigh-bone. It was futile. I just knew I wanted to go home. So I reached for the phone, my only anchor to a world where I had felt healthier and could hold on to a coherent thought. For once, it was in easy reach where I tried to keep it, under my pillows, not hidden in acres of rolling, hospital-cornered linens or a million miles away on top of the dizzyingly high bedside cabinet.

*

'Can I come home?' I pleaded, my despair flooding the line and pouring out through the earpiece into our 15th Street apartment.

There was nothing Beth wanted more for me, or her. But someone had to be the grown-up. Although my pleas were tearing her up, my anguish was corralled by the power of her reassuring voice. Mature and complex, flecked with the dark deposits of a life well-lived, her voice had been smoothed by youthful experience earned through serious thoughts about how to live that life.

'It's late, honey. You have to get your rest. I'll take you home soon, I promise. You'll see me first thing in the morning.'

Nights were a challenge. I was the kid threatened by the noises of the night-time house. Every cooling creak was an intimation of unknown terror. Every settling sound, a signal of a monstrous uncurling limb. Except, the threats here seemed more real. The hard railing of the bed pushed incessantly against my unfeeling arm. The vague sensation of discomfort was worse than pain. Was that muffled feeling the agony of gagged nerves screaming?

The corridors outside the ward bore a command in red, hexagonal injunction: *QUIET. Patients are healing.*

The bawling capital letters couldn't be heard over the endless activity of the hospital, however. When I tried to recoup lost sleep, after Tenko's morning ablutions and between therapy sessions, my day was broken up like a plane journey interrupted by drinks, meals, announcements, duty free carts. The passengers couldn't be allowed to become listless. Breakfast. Doctors' rounds. The long needle delivering abdominal injections of the Heparin that protected me from the blood clot that could finish me off. Lunch. Alfonso's hollering television shows. Dinner. And, less structured but more structural, the on-going renovations of HJD.

'Either someone's got a hell of a lot of pressure on their

brain,' I thought, 'or they need to calm down with the fucking incessant drilling upstairs.'

At apparently random intervals throughout the day, jackhammers would pound in mocking derision of the six-sided sign that demanded quiet. Then eventually, our lights would be dimmed.

Nights weren't always better. In addition to the regular moans of my fellow patients and my own night-time fears, on the night of 15th November, Alfonso's family descended en masse. For someone so particular about his sleeping arrangements, The Wee Man and his family were remarkably blasé about anyone else's ability to get some kip. I fumed silently, not wishing to poison Room 920's well, or spur the Dallier clan on to further heights of raucous rage against the dying of the light. I muted my complaints, not least, because of my eternal gratitude to The Wee Man for handling my first day fall so well.

The next morning, the cause for all the hubbub was revealed. During a merciful lull in the infirmary's attentions, Alfonso approached my bed.

'I am leaving this morning,' he told me. 'Goodbye. And good luck. To you and your wife.'

His farewell was fond and tender, and I basked in it. It wasn't a time for technical quibbles about marital status. I was getting to see another side of my room-mate.

'Thank you, Alfonso,' I said. 'I hope everything goes well. For you and your family. That's a nice bunch of kids you have. You must be very proud. Wish them all the best for me.'

Alfonso was being shipped out to a sub-acute facility. A place that fell somewhere between HJD and a nursing home. Sub-acute programmes cater primarily for patients who are in the initial stages of recovery and aren't ready for the hard work of rehab, as well as those who have completed acute rehabilitation and are ready to step it down a notch.

Arguably, The Wee Man shouldn't have been under the care of the Rusk Institute in the first place. To be assigned to Rusk, a patient has to fall within a narrow slot of disability. They must be damaged enough to require intensive rehabilitation but have enough potential to benefit from three or more hours of rehabilitation a day, and have the ability to put in those hours. There had been much discussion of where I was on this spectrum before the ambulance had been assigned to take me out of Methodist Hospital.

Even in the aftermath of his stroke, Alfonso was the picture of a spry, compact senior. His age weighed against an expansive upside, though. He wasn't minded to tolerate the fussing whippersnappers of various ages, or throw himself wholeheartedly into some kind of Stroke Dance Revolution or cybernetic reinvention. He hadn't been happy in HJD. As far as he was concerned, anything would have been better. Now that he was being released and would no longer be 'treated like a bird!' – one of his favourite, most incomprehensible complaints – he could let his fortress of fury subside a little.

Rusk had been great for me, and I was continuing to make great strides in my physical recovery. My medical team had begun to talk with Beth about what apparatus I would need on my release. Top of the list, I would need my very own cane. Hearing this was yet another moment driving home like the pounding tools above that nothing would be quite the same again. I had gone to bed on 30th September as a young man. The next time I saw that bed, I would be a cane-carrying oldster. Fortunately, Beth was modifying the narrative for me. She took out the iPad and we browsed through pages of alternative walking sticks.

'I can't decide what I want,' I told her as we leafed through the options on the screen. 'I'm torn between supa dupa fly and Order of the Thistle.'

'Like a swordstick?' she asked. 'I looked into that. They're banned in a couple of states, and in a bunch of others they're treated as concealed or disguised weapons. In Britain, you can't even sell them unless they're antique.'

'Cool! I'd rather have an antique one, anyway.' But we both knew a swordstick wouldn't fly.

As Beth continued, my disappointment was quickly forgotten. 'Oh! I saw a good one!' she told me, and brought up a picture on the iPad. This brass-handled cane would have been at home supporting Edwyn Collins at The Rock Shop. Easily. Its specifications indicated that the cane could support up to 250lb, while a typical person exerts no more than 100lb on their cane. Attractive as the stick was, this wasn't even the main selling point. The top of the cane screwed off to reveal five thin, 2oz, hardened-glass flasks, or around six to eight shots of booze. How impossibly sophisticated!

Soon enough, I took delivery of the actual cane I was to take home. It was a facsimile of the functional, unfabulous walking assistance instrument that Steph had been teaching me to use in physical therapy. When it arrived, an instructional leaflet swung from the handle, depicting a happy cripple of indeterminate gender in chinos, a pair of white sneakers and youthful old age. This undercut the trade name that was presented in a fashionable, caps-free, Ryan Gosling-evoking font that spoke of the existentially cool delivery of sex and violence – *drive*. Nevertheless, we somehow invested this symbol of my infirmity with youthful humour. Our pal Neal visited and directed me how to properly shake my new toy at the young uns who would have to 'Get orff my lawn!' He showed me the photo he took of me practicing, depicting a cartoonish curmudgeon. Scanning from head to toe, left to right along the bed, I saw an army crop that barely hid the holes in the head, a pair of sixties-era Michael Caine frames, a patchy, amateurishly shaved beard that outlined a face contorted in mock rage, and a left arm that held the stick and curled against a royal blue T-shirt clinging to a skinny core. Hospital tags had been pushed half-way up the forearm so they wouldn't flap around. The picture was rounded off by a spindly right leg folded underneath the figure. There was a slogan on the royal blue T-shirt:

KEEP CALM AND REVERSE THE POLARITY

Doctor Who! The figure was me! I was pleasantly surprised to find that the shocking and ugly elements knitted together to form a guy who looked . . . OK. In a way. He certainly seemed to have a sense of humour about his situation. I thought I could grow to like him.

Over the next couple of days, the other items that had been recommended to Beth and I from a short list of disability aids arrived, together with notice that their insurance-reduced costs had been applied to our credit card bill. They all bore that same sophisticated, modern script. The two grab bars for the shower. The lightweight wheelchair. Meanwhile, Steph's cane-wielding lessons continued in the gym. As I learned to use it on the gym's miniature staircase, I came to the conclusion that I either missed my old room-mate, or I was suffering from PTSD, because across the room, a guy with the same name as The Wee Man was taking instruction, and I was quite *verklempt*.

I hadn't seen much of Alfonso's successor in Room 920. The curtain around his bed was pulled closed most of the time. When it wasn't, I still had difficulty manoeuvring in bed in order to be able to see him. What I could piece together from scraps of conversation was that Bill Keller was in his eighties. Heavily-rotated discussions of urinary issues and the slurping of hot drinks confirmed the fact. Was this the future we were fighting so hard for? Well, not exactly. Still, the voice behind the curtain conveyed a vim that belied Bill's years.

'These young people who are looking after me really are very good,' he told a visitor one day. 'Very knowledgeable and enthusiastic.'

Bill wasn't ready to do much therapy out of his bed yet, so his occupational therapist came to him.

'What would you like to focus on, Mr Keller?' she asked.

'I'd like to be able to return to work when I'm finished here.'

In his eighties! Good for you, Bill! Or not. I wasn't sure anymore.

He explained to his therapist that he intended to resume his business as an investment adviser once he had recovered from the brain surgery and resulting complications that had occasioned his stay in HJD. He was concerned that the trouble he was having with writing would make this difficult.

'OK, Mr Keller. Here's a pen and a pad. Can you write a sentence for me?'

Bill complied, and the therapist read the result

' "I love Paula." That's lovely. And who is Paula?'

Paula was Bill's second wife. He adored her, and it became clear she loved him, too. Paula was in HJD with a frequency that rivalled Beth's, often with friends and family in tow. While we discussed 'What Bling Cane Would Biggie Choose,' the conversations behind the Kellers' curtain reflected the more mature concerns of the sort of people who split their time between Manhattan's well-to-do Upper East Side and the privileged enclaves of Westchester County. The latest books receiving coverage in the *New York Times*. The economy and property prices. Renovations to apartments and summer homes. Also, in the aftermath of Hurricane Sandy, yard clean-up.

Paula and Bill's friend Joyce, a lady of stentorian tone and similar vintage to the Kellers, had strident views on this last topic and the failings of a ne'er-do-well nephew or neighbour or neighbour's nephew called Hank. 'I *mean!*' she exclaimed in an exasperated tone, 'Two weeks have passed, and that damned tree is still lying in his front yard.'

'Really?' Paula responded. 'We just had our tree guy come and take care of ours. Would you like us to pass along his number?'

Not previously having been aware of the seriousness of these issues, I fixed Beth with a concerned look. I had a terrible admission to make. So grim, it could only be whispered in the shadows of Joyce's booming condemnations. 'I don't even *have* a tree guy.'

The mockery was affectionate though, and when Paula emerged from behind the divider to offer the remains of the pumpkin pie and cream Joyce had brought, we cheerfully accepted. A companionable, chewing silence fell over a room filled with late autumn light and the spicy fragrance of the pie.

Bill was still an octogenarian, though. The next day, having delivered and tidied away my laundry, massaged my left hand, and tended my febrile mind, Beth was getting ready to leave and take the subway back to Brooklyn when Bill said, 'Excuse me, young lady. Would you call the nurse for me?'

Like Alfonso, Bill had led a life in which tasks not directly related to salary were attended to by a convenient helpmate. If Paula was absent, my partner would have to do. Tired by the demands of the past six weeks and distracted by the flesh collapsing into the void left by Bill's absent mass of skull bone, Beth didn't mention the call button hanging from Bill's bed, but dutifully retrieved another woman from the hallway. Then she dashed back into the room to bid me farewell before she made her escape.

Meanwhile, the preparations for my release continued. Notwithstanding the cane selection process, it was a serious business. At the time, I didn't register the depth of my carers' concerns, only the kindness of that concern. If we hadn't lived in a single-storey apartment in an elevator building, if Beth hadn't been able to take a month off work to make sure

I didn't ignite fat fires, I would have been transferred to the step-down facility with Alfonso. Nevertheless, progress was good.

A week previously, in the first of two Saturday PT sessions, Steph had re-administered a STREAM test, or STroke REhabilitation Assessment of Movement. This involved a repetition of certain of thirty tasks that I was told had been measured soon after my arrival at Rusk. Over twenty minutes, I was asked to perform movements spread among upper-limb movements, lower limb movements and basic mobility actions. Steph compared the range and success of my movements to the results of the original test, and declared herself happy with my progress.

Things went well enough that when I expressed my jealousy of the older lady on my left, who was being encouraged to mimic what her therapist called a 'soccer' player, despite her evident distrust of such commie bullshit, Steph promised me a football in our next session.

The fifteenth of November was a red-letter day. I got to push a football around with my left foot. Steph declared that we were down to fine-tuning my cane-assisted walking on the same day that Bioness, the maker of my favourite cyber-conversion tools, followed me on Twitter. Around the same time, another alert popped up on my phone. It probably wasn't to be advised, but it was tempting. Groupon.com wanted me to sign up for a four-hour BMW 328i reservation to celebrate my release. I mean, it was only a little tempting – my occupational therapists and nurses had taught me well – but I welcomed the feeling of tantalisation. 'I'm alive, you bastards!' I thought.

Dawn brought round some more CDs that offered guided relaxation and ambient sounds that I could take home. One promised 'no jarring tempo changes or unexpected interruptions'. I was grateful, even as I told Dawn that jarring tempo changes were exactly the sort of thing I liked. Although I had an improving sense of time, and the days no longer disappeared the way they so recently had, they still airily evaporated as we accelerated towards my discharge. Towards deliverance.

On 19th November, there was a big event. Joe paid a visit with his partner Claudia later in the day, and I told them all about it. Effortlessly handsome and successful, they were still happy to step out of a Ralph Lauren advert to visit a sick pal, and I was enjoying their visit.

'Beth brought my going home pants this morning!'

I happily brandished a pair of boxer briefs in Beth's favourite colour. Joe snorted.

'The best part about forgetting you're Scottish is that your definition of "pants" is the funny one.'

After they left, I embarked upon a marathon physical therapy session with Michelle in charge. We started with a pair of light dumb-bells. Their purpose was to encourage concentration and form, I think, because my left arm already felt like it weighed a tonne. Nevertheless, it was exciting to be doing something new. Something that regular folks did.

I finished the set, and my therapist dropped the encouraging chatter for a moment to resume our conversation. 'So, you're leaving us tomorrow?'

'The day after, actually. Just in time for Thanksgiving.'

The holiday was rapidly approaching and today, Monday, was my last inpatient PT session.

'OK,' Michelle said. 'Do you want to go outside?'

Did I ever! A shiver of Stockholm syndrome whistled through my skinny scaffold, but was blown out by the thought of being able to report my exploits to Beth later that evening. Michelle and I stopped briefly at Room 920 so I could put more clothes on, then I sticked my way down the now familiar corridor to the elevator bank while she blocked for me. It took forever for the lift to come. I was so close to being outside – properly this time – but still. The waiting.

Bing!

We commiserated briefly with our fellow inmates and wardens about the time we had to spend waiting to move between floors, and I was reminded of one of the truths of a long hospital stay: eventually, you're going to find yourself chatting with someone redolent of that particular smell of ammonia. In HJD, this was all the more marked because we would forget to drink or couldn't be bothered to drink or couldn't reach our water glasses or lift our jugs. For all these reasons, our urine was more concentrated, pungent.

Eventually, we were able to vacate the elevator. I was dressed for the outside, but still surprised by the actual, physical wind invading the lobby. A season had passed me by, but when we passed through the doors – thin, momentous sheets of glass – it was confirmed. Winter was rushing in.

The sky was blue, though, so when Michelle asked how far I thought I could manage, we decided to walk south down Second Avenue where it bisected Stuyvesant Square park, surrounded by nature in the Flatiron District. In my excitement, I forgot how to negotiate the stairs outside the lobby with a stick.

'Stop and think about that for a second, Ricky.'

My stride had the yips, and I couldn't quite figure out what to do next. Michelle gave me time to figure it out for myself. Standing at the top of the steps, I really had no idea. All I could figure out was that I must have been doing something the wrong way round. In the excitement of being outside, I was trying to start with my cane, then my strong leg, then the weak leg. That's the technique I made the effort to burn into my mind for stairs. *Climbing* stairs. The steps outside the huge glassy panes *descended* from the concrete expanse to the pavement. I was doing everything the wrong way round. I gingerly laid my left hand on the handrail. Because of the damage to my brain, it didn't register the steely chill.

My more functional right arm reached out and extended the triangular foot of the cane down onto the step way below. Positioning my weight squarely over my right leg, I let my other leg slap onto the stair before readjusting and following with the stronger leg. Once again, I recalibrated.

My right arm reached out again and extended the triangular foot of the cane down onto the second step. Positioning my weight squarely over my right leg, I let my other leg slap onto the stair before readjusting and following with the stronger leg. Once again, I recalibrated.

One more. It was beginning to feel natural. Was that a good thing? My right arm reached out and extended the triangular foot of the cane down onto the sidewalk level. Positioning my weight squarely over my right leg, I let my other leg slap onto the pavement before readjusting and following with the stronger leg. Once again, I recalibrated and tried to figure out what was next. Looking past the MRI truck, a steady stream of traffic was flowing along 17th Street.

Michelle and I made our way to the crosswalk at the corner and I managed a further block before we had to turn back. I wouldn't be doing a lot of walking any time soon. This was another cold blast of reality, but my optimism hadn't been dulled by my final inpatient PT session. We retraced our steps and I shuffled back up the steps. Up the elevator again, and as we approached Room 920, Michelle suggested that we finish our session at the gym. It was quiet now. Steph and Rodney were chatting, as if passing the time while waiting for someone.

'Hi, Ricky! You've been busy! You looking forward to going home?'

'I can't wait!'

'Right. Well, we'd better get your picture for the Hall of Fame, then.'

Now I really was ready to go home. In the picture with my therapists that adorns the gym, my smile still looks a little lop-sided, if you know what you're looking for. It's real, though, and I appear trim and fit and, after over fifty-two excruciating daily stomach injections, more than ready to go home.

Of course, the camera sometimes lies.

At 6a.m. on 21st November, Tenko dragged me out of bed for my shower. When speech therapy started at 10, I was already bushed. It didn't matter, though. Liat's visit to my bedside was mostly social, filling in the time until Beth would arrive to take me home. My partner, the subway nerd, knew that negotiating the streets to the Third Avenue subway station, with its crowds and turnstiles, then barrelling along on the L to Lorimer Street in Brooklyn before walking to Metropolitan Avenue to change to the G was desperately ambitious. The G was a locomotive disaster, even for the able-bodied and right-minded. It was the only non-shuttle service in the MTA system that didn't run through Manhattan and as such, had to cede precedence to its cousin, the F. Even at rush hour, the G was only scheduled to run every ten, or even twelve minutes. It would only take a minor delay, then Beth would be looking after a newly released stroke patient on a crowded platform for quarter of an hour.

Stuff had been happening during my confinement. Not just Hurricane Sandy and a presidential election. The Uber car service had been getting some traction in New York. Having had access to my law firm's car services until immediately before my stroke, we had never had call to call them, but our tech-minded MBA-toting friends loved the tech-utilising venture-funded start-up.

This was how we found ourselves sitting in the lobby of HJD, peering at Beth's iPhone. We were meant to be able to watch the car on the map on the phone as it made its way to us. What we were actually watching was a static dot, and our excitement was waning. Thirty minutes after the appointed hour, Beth managed to connect with our driver and explain our situation.

So it was that, over an hour late, I was using my Sonoko-taught method for getting into a car. I got as close to the passenger doorway as possible, and sat down, perpendicular to the sidewalk, before swinging my legs into our ride. Then we sat in traffic for another hour and a half.

In the end, we weren't happy to get to our apartment, just exhausted. I suppose we should have been glad to get home at all. Around that time, the city admitted that almost a third of the nineteen thousand lane miles of road that covered the five boroughs of New York City and conveyed cars like misfiring neurons jerking and halting through sticky streets were substandard. But still, almost three million cars would scramble across forty-seven structurally deficient bridges rated 'fracture critical'. We could have tried to take that G train, but more than a third of the mainline signals had exceeded their useful life. Maintenance workers would build their own replacement parts, because after more than fifty years, manufacturers no longer made them.

I turned to Beth in the car, and remembered an old refrain of mine. 'I love this city, but it just doesn't work.'

All this stuff was bad enough, but I was reminded of the unspoken fear that New York was always teetering on the brink of tragedy.

It had been on an autumn morning – a Tuesday – during the early days of my first marriage that I had been flying back from attending a wedding in Stockholm. A seasoned traveller, I had ignored the safety presentations and simply surreptitiously and superstitiously felt for the lifejacket under the seat. It was a transatlantic flight like any one of the dozens I had taken, and the details of the witchcraft of flight were of no interest. I don't even remember, now, what film I was watching when, an hour or so off the east coast of the United States, the pilot's voice came over the intercom.

'As you've probably noticed, the cabin crew have lowered the blinds.'

I hadn't noticed. This was in the days when it wasn't worth paying attention to all of the hundreds of forgettable little events that might occur during the course of an eight-hour flight from Stockholm to New York. The sun had been pouring in the port windows of the cabin. Passengers had wanted to sleep, watch their movies.

'Also, we've turned the aircraft around 180 degrees.'

With the blinds closed, this manoeuvre had been executed smoothly. If the blinds had been opened again, we would have seen a world flipped around, with the southerly sun shining in from the starboard side. US airspace had been closed, the pilot told us. As a child of the Cold War and the survivor of hundreds of imagined nuclear holocausts, I had remained unruffled, and flicked through the in-flight magazine; there were any number of groundless fears that might have given rise to our diversion. Maybe I could catch another movie, I had thought. What was the point in worrying? We would be on the ground soon enough.

Then the next piece of information, delivered in the same calm voice of a pilot who had guided 180 tonnes of Airbus over the oceans more times than he would care to remember, gave me pause.

'Canadian airspace is also closed, so we've been instructed to head back to Shannon.'

Shannon, I knew from my work in aviation finance, was the most westerly airport in Europe and like a parking lot for planes. The closest airport, if you have to turn tail and flee the United States. The fears of decades ago resurfaced. Had some sort of contretemps in the Middle East rippled to the Jewish capital of the western world? Or maybe one of the reactors at Indian Point had melted down. Unit 2 was just a few weeks over twenty-seven years old. It was due to enter its 'period of extended operation' a little under twelve years after the date of our flight.

A little less than eight hours after flight UA69 had turned around off the east coast, we touched down in the verdant oasis of County Clare. Around one hundred Swedes flipped open their impossibly sleek Ericsson cell phones.

My fears weren't decades old any more. The date was 11th September 2001, and as we were driven in a coach along the darkening roads that split ancient fields and balanced on the edge of cliffs, my ex-wife's office was as one with hundreds of thousands of tonnes of toxic dust blowing across Manhattan and the Hudson River.

There was nothing to say. We rode in silence.

Years later, New Yorkers still talked about how the city changed that day. Amid the terrible loss, burned into the city's consciousness like the falling figure frozen on the screen of the television set in my room in a Clare hotel, there was a coming together that could never lightly be put aside, in the city at least. Two years later, when the August 2003 blackout occurred, it was free of the arson, looting and vandalism that had marked the 1977 outage.

Fast forward to the day I returned home from HJD, and the cargo facilities at JFK airport in Queens were forty years old. Almost two-thirds of those facilities were unfit for modern screening, storage and distribution. Not everything had changed.

I had started frequenting Harry Boland's in May 2007. I had gotten back to Park Slope late one night following an intimate LCD Soundsystem gig at the old, club-like, Studio B in Greenpoint. I was, I suppose, the ageing hipster of their song 'Losing My Edge', made flesh.

I had moderated my home-listening habits away from the jarring tempo changes and unexpected interruptions that I would one day mention to Dawn the recreational therapist, but there was still little opportunity for procuring pleasure from music in my old, loveless apartment. Fortunately, Andy the Barman – who was all about Primus and Alice Donut and jarring tempo changes – would let me bring in mixes to be loaded into the jukebox. I'd cheat a little bit by finishing the CDs with a long, extended track that would stretch out my dollars.

I would sit at the end of the bar, far from the jukie, near the door. New York was a mess. My apartment was a mess. And here I was, with my people. The retired rent boy who miaowed and spat like a cat so he wouldn't have to chat with the squares, but who in the right mood would discuss the art classes he took to refine his painting skills. The *Economist*-devouring ex-air force man who was chased down a bottle by the ghosts of abusive priests. The men and women who didn't care if my facade was crumbling to reveal the toxins in the structure beneath. The last, apocalyptic chords of one of those extended tracks, 'New York I Love You, But You're Bringing Me Down', built and climbed the walls.

I didn't know it yet, but maybe, just maybe, from somewhere out of that unpromising scene, things were eventually going to work out OK. Maybe Beth and I would help each other through, with or without New York.

14

Thanksgiving

The morning after I got home from the Hospital for Joint Diseases, we woke up early, still tired. It was Thanksgiving Day. Family time in the United States, and we had a lot to be thankful for. The prospect of non-hospital food was a relief, and I was ready for a grand feast. Beth's parents had come to town to celebrate with us, since we couldn't make it down to South Carolina.

Beth was my new shower helper, and in the tradition of her predecessor Tenko, she was a hard taskmaster. Upon waking up in my own bed for the first time in almost two months, still tired from the cab ride and eating pizza out with Kathy and Ray Monahan, I had been limited to an extra five minutes in bed before my shower.

It passed quickly.

The bathroom wasn't quite the same as the image I had tried to paint from memory. The walls were dotted with the grab bars that had been sourced by the hospital and installed by Paul's guy, and a plastic bath seat sat under the shower head. After escorting me to the bathroom and before helping me arrange my body on the chair, Beth insisted that I check out my shrunken frame in the mirror shower as part of 'normalisation'. I didn't recognise it at all.

I had already been recommending the stroke diet to people. 'I lost 35lb!' I would beam, but my muscle tone was horrible. As my rediscovery of my body had progressed, a sense of judgement had returned. It was a good thing that I couldn't twist my body for a better view, because my arse looked like it had fallen off. Where my buttocks used to be, there was just a vertical, alien continuation where my back met my thighs. I was glad to move on from that part of the ritual, and, soon, with a minimum of fuss, my ablutions were completed.

The best part was being dried. Shuffling from bed to bath seat, I barely felt like a man, but I felt like a prince when Beth carefully and tenderly dried my body. Heck, for better or worse, I finally felt as well cared for as Sean Connery in *You Only Live Twice*. Then, drier than I had ever been able to dry myself, before or after, I sat on the edge of the bed again. Dressing myself was my own task.

We had laid out my clothes for the day on the bed before the shower, in such an order that I could dress myself as Sonoko had instructed. They were loose-fitting, because loose clothes were easier to slip in and out of. In fact, everything was loose-fitting now. With each item, I used my right arm to dress my left side first. For the long-sleeve T-shirt, I started by putting my weak arm in its sleeve. After pulling the shirt over the arm and my head, wriggling my right arm into the other sleeve was no problem. My left hand was able to hold my jeans button steady while the fingers of my right hand manoeuvred the eye over and around it. With a little help with my socks and a pair of trainers, I was ready before our odd little family began to assemble. First to arrive was Sparky, with the other Sparkies – dad, brother and sister-in-law.

As a healthcare professional – a type more venerated than ever in our post-stroke household – and in light of his help when my stroke hit, Sparky got an even warmer welcome than usual. Becoming a doctor in New York is a gruelling task. A fellow denizen of Harry Boland's bar was training at Maimonides Medical Center in Brooklyn. There, six patients were treated per square foot per year, gabbling in an assortment of the eight hundred – *eight hundred* – languages spoken in New York City. The experiences she would describe recalled nothing so much as the experiences of the cadets pushed through R. Lee Ermey's sadistic Marine Corps training in the first act of *Full Metal Jacket*. Except there was more blood at Maimonides, obviously.

Medical school graduates were subjected to sleep deprivation and left to sink or swim. Broken down and rebuilt as doctors. Sparky's training had seen him pass through the emergency rooms of Maimo, Kings County, St John's and Long Island College hospitals. In the two years I had known him, he had fallen asleep at the wheel of his car after another multiple-shift marathon more times than he could count. To the admitting doctor who had attended to my stroke, and Sparky who cleaned up afterwards, I was an anomaly of medical science, but I was not special. Though they should be special to us.

Sparky had arrived early, relishing a day off. He had to be early, because he had brought the turkey. He got it set up and headed out to collect more supplies while I was left with the kindergartener's task of stuffing sweet peppers with goats' cheese using a blunt spoon. While Sparky was buying the ingredients for the seven-layer dip with which he would celebrate Thanksgiving, Hanukkah, Christmas, Purim, Easter and birthdays, Paul and his Jen arrived with their ten-year-old Muppet-loving moppet, Jill.

We were particularly fond of Jill. In a complicated world of overwork, blood, shit, vomit and death, she saw Beth and I the way we felt – like a couple of teenagers hopelessly in love. Admittedly, this was partly because *everyone* over twelve was unimaginably old to Jill. Still, when she would organise the guests at a party, she was always careful to sit us together. Perhaps our placings would be marked by a drawing of a couple in a kilt and a long, white dress. When

Beth would forget her gloves after a dinner, Jill would point out that something has been left behind by 'the girl from Bethandricky'.

For Thanksgiving, Jill came in bearing two new pieces of artwork to celebrate my return from the dead: a welcome home banner and a T-shirt proclaiming, 'I ♥ SROKS'. Appropriately, this was probably how I would have spelled 'strokes' at that moment, too. Once these offerings had been presented, we discussed Jill's recent foot injury and made plans for our hotly anticipated walker-race in the common hallway.

Dinner was another step on the path back to normality. Jen and Paul had brought the sides. Ray and Kathy arrived with the wine. The food was delicious; everyone had left their burning barrels of turkey-frying oil at home. Admittedly, the whole event had been catered and cleared by our friends and family, but still: we had hosted a social event on the first day of the rest of our lives. Despite creeping exhaustion, Beth had been hilarious and charming for at least twelve straight hours after entertaining Kathy and Ray last night, too.

Beth, Geronimo and Seamus and Cyclops, and Ray and Kathy and Jen and Paul and Jill and the Sparkies had all come together for Thanksgiving. It turned out that, three thousand miles from home, you could choose your friends *and* your family.

Beth – my immediate family – told the assembled company how she had made it through the past two months. 'He had no idea where he was, or who he was,' she explained, 'but he was really funny. I mean, I didn't want to laugh too much, in case he thought I was laughing *at* him, but that did make it a lot easier.'

It was nice to hear that, even when I was stripped down to pure id, my girlfriend thought I was funny. Even if she was actually laughing at me a bunch of the time because I was a ridiculous man. Even better, in this reduced state, I had a chance to rebuild myself, maybe even improve myself in some ways.

I'd never claim to be the Messiah, but my fifty-one days and nights in hospital had served much the same purpose as the biblical forty days and nights of the prophets: the stroke ward had isolated me from the temptations, corruptions and softness of comfortable society. Methodist Hospital of the New York Presbyterian Healthcare System, then the New York University Langone Medical Center at the Hospital for Joint Diseases, had acted as places of purgation, or an entry to the Buddha's threefold way.

The fourth century saint, John the Ascetic, told the story of a hermit who found that the desert was not the best place to achieve contemplation, because of the resulting preoccupation with meeting one's material needs and the tendency to marvel at one's own spiritual achievements. Total isolation may inflate the ego, while remaining in society counteracts that tendency. The moral was that solitude may be better achieved in community, where material needs are provided for and the seeker is more humble.

The stroke ward did serve more than just traditional medical needs, in that it provided a place of solitude; that is to say, the philosophical concept of solitude. Not solitude as in being alone, but a state of mind in which I could still hear the voices of society, allowing an opportunity for deep contemplation and self-examination. As in the desert, life had been pared down to the bone. I was dependent on what was made available to me in order to survive. At the same time, I had been within a community in the truest sense. A team of nurses and orderlies had provided for my material needs around the clock. To round it off, you've got to be humble when you're wearing a Texas catheter and someone else has to wipe your arse.

Thanksgiving was a success, but Beth and I were still jet-lagged from the past two months, what with my exile from natural light and her forty-eight-hour days of hospital visits, work and piss-soaked laundry. Regardless, she was able to slowly help me achieve a limited independence. Eventually the administrators at Langone arranged for me to be visited by the Visiting Nurse Service of New York. The first nurse that they provided came round and passed me to start home therapy, even though my blood pressure readings still hadn't been entirely stabilised.

On 6th December, our alarms started to go off at around 8a.m., interspersed with phone calls. I picked up my phone to switch off the alarm, and on swiping the screen found myself talking to a nice young man who identified himself as Ranjan, the outpatient physical therapist. He was calling to let me know that he had plans to come by for an initial session between 9 and 10.

I discovered that, for some reason, VNS visits were set up like ambushes. For example, I might have received a call along these lines: 'Hi. It's your nurse. I'm on the corner. See you in five . . . Reschedule . . . ? Well, we can do it in a couple of months, if you prefer.'

On the day of Ranjan's first visit, this was how I interpreted his message:

'Hi. Your nurse here. It's 8a.m. I assume you can have your strokey ass up and showered and dressed in workout clothes and fed in time for a physical therapy session between 9 and 10a.m.?'

Well, I was pretty desperate to get to the Rusk building in Midtown and get on the outpatient rehabilitation programme, so sure, I could do that. By 10, I had showered myself on my little bath chair, gotten on something loose enough to work out in – which, for my new model skinny ass, could have been anything from the tuxedo I got at 17 to the Brooklyn Industries pants I actually chose to wear, the button of which had been under critical threat one stroke and 35lb ago – brushed my teeth, had a cup of tea, devoured a bowl of

Special K, buzzed up someone I assumed was the therapist, and sat through half an hour of Fox 5's local *Good Morning New York* show.

Superstorm Sandy was still dominating the news. Also, the guy who played J. Peterman on Seinfeld was promoting Take Your Pet to Work Day. He mentioned that all NY hospitals were allowing dog therapy now. Dawn had certainly brought round cute dogs for Alfonso and me to reject on a regular basis. I was allergic. The Wee Man no doubt thought that they would attack him in his sleep if they could get a hold of his scent, and devour his soul. Dawn would no doubt have trained them to do so happily.

Yep, it was definitely time to find out what had happened to Ranjan.

It turned out that he was alive and answering his phone, and expected to be with me in five-to-ten minutes. This was also standard procedure, and I understood, I really did. The VNS didn't want their nurses standing around on cold New York corners all day waiting for the lame, crippled and injured to get their shit together while they could be tending to other lame, crippled and injured patients. So the patients waited for them. This cripple, however, had sat through *Good Morning New York*, and was damned if he was going to continue to sit through the morning chat shows, too.

Thank god, Ranjan finally arrived. He had me show him the exercises I'd been given to do at home. Then we got down to work, and I remembered why I enjoyed physical therapy so much. For the past two and a half weeks, I had been given no benchmarks against which I could measure my progress, other than a vague sense of 'I couldn't have done that a couple of weeks ago' that was pretty easily offset by the feeling of 'Bloody Hell, my left arm feels vaguely sore/tingly/numb today. I don't have a clear sense of it feeling like that a month ago.'

Without therapy, and my inpatient therapy log, I didn't remember that I couldn't even raise my arm above my waist a month ago. So, as requested, I stood steady in a variety of poses with my eyes open, then closed. I walked a few yards, picking up items strategically left on the floor. I showed off my uncanny ability to get in the shower and sit on, and get up off, the toilet. I got onto the bed and rolled over.

'Like,' I could imagine Alfonso saying, 'a dog.'

Ranjan and I hit the internal fire stairs and I demonstrated my ability to get up and down a flight of steps, only being slightly thrown off by the fact that, unlike hospitals, regular buildings only have a handrail on one side. As soon as I had negotiated maybe my fifth set of stairs in two months, we headed back to the flat to take a blood pressure reading. It had spiked a bit, but still, I was in a good mood. My competitive inner child was doing cartwheels, the show off.

When we finished the session, Ranjan pronounced himself satisfied with what he had seen, and asked what my aims were for outpatient PT. I told him, with Beth – my real audience, sitting a few feet away, that I wanted to get back to normal, pre-stroke, 100 per cent functionality. He said he reckoned that was reasonable, which suggested to me that he hadn't read my records. Then he outlined his expectations regarding a couple of weeks of home PT prior to sending me to Rusk Midtown, and we had a quick chat about setting up Access-a-Ride, the city's paratransit service, for the trips. I got a copy of Ranjan's business card, including the VNS main office details so I could address that with the head nurse for my case.

Then it was right back to regular strokiness. Within ten minutes of Ranjan's departure, I had no idea where the business card was. Still, I had been using the most useful piece of advice I got in speech therapy (memory section) and was keeping all the new information I might need in my phone, so the physical therapist's personal details had already been added prior to business card loss. I called him and got the additional details for the main office. 'Yay for the positive results of therapy!' I thought.

It was agreed with the VNS that another step on the path to normality would be reinstating my daughter's visits. These were quite limited at first, because in a New York neighbourhood where kids were ferried from gym class to power tools camp to the tennis courts to a wacky science educator before lunch, stroke survivors were *boring*.

Nevertheless, in anticipation of this new normal, Linda popped round to see how I was doing. She brought a decaf coffee and a pastry for each of us, and sat down at our little black dinner table that teetered on spindly little iron legs. She told me I was looking well, and that she was glad I was home. After some brief questions regarding my current welfare, counsel moved on to more substantive matters. For the first time, I coherently formed an awareness of watching my brain from a third-person remove. I didn't want to say anything stupid. Make any incorrect plans. Give up anything that might have been taken down and used in evidence against me. Yet I was still keenly aware of what was later diagnosed as the ravaging of my processing speed. Around half of people think that memory works like a video recorder. If that's the case, my measurable decline in processing speed was like capturing images at a rate of a frame every thirty seconds through a scratched and scarred lens. Not only was my damaged brain doing a hobbled sprint to keep up with the conversation, it was doubling its workload as it sat on its own shoulder, monitoring.

'There's no way I'm going to remember any of this. Do you mind if I take some notes?' I asked.

'Oh, I'm not going to get into much. You won't need to do that.'

You have no idea.

Within twenty seconds, I was flailing and had to ask again. After acceding to my request, Linda completed her information dump with all due haste and headed to work.

That evening, Beth got home from work and asked how the meeting went.

'Er, quite well, I think? She started off all sweetness and light. Something about how I'd reverted to the nice guy she'd met back in the late nineties. I think that was meant to be a compliment about how my base personality is actually quite pleasant. I'm not sure how I'm meant to feel about my brain-damaged, reliant, subjugated self being so much preferable to the hateful, functional me! After that, it was all business. She's got some ideas about when we can look after Elizabeth. Let me get my notes.'

I made a hobbling round trip to the kitchen table, returning with paper in hand. I sat down, and started reciting the notes with increasing horror. My handwriting wasn't that good before the stroke. After winning the school handwriting prize for primary four when I was nine, my script had been assaulted by years of legal study and practice. Now, the spindly, crippled scrawl of my left hand was truly illegible. The words I could painfully decipher didn't trigger any recollections.

Beth called Linda to let her know that we hadn't been able to assemble the content of the conversation. They agreed that Elizabeth would have a quick visit on Wednesday evening, and Beth told Linda her that if there were any arrangements to be made, it would be best if she sent an email, or Beth was present at the time.

Elizabeth began to spend Wednesday evenings and half a weekend day with Beth and me, as we started building up visitation again. Despite her tendency to anxiety in the face of less serious issues, Elizabeth showed the same resilience in the face of my stroke that she had displayed when the permanence of her parents' separation became clear. She took on additional small chores without complaint, and was more receptive to instruction while I was still clearly damaged and the dark days of autumn were fresh in everyone's minds.

During one visit, I asked her about what differences she had noticed having a Stroke Dad. Not too much, she told me, though she did feel she was having to take on a little more responsibility.

'I'm reading a new book,' Elizabeth told me. She was a voracious reader. 'It's called *The Book of Blood and Shadow*. It's about this high schooler, Nora, and she's doing work for The Hoff. The Hoff's a professor, and he has a stroke. She spends a bunch of time visiting him in hospital.'

'Really? Does the author get down what it's like?'

'Yeah, it's pretty well done.'

'Cool,' I told her, and added a request. 'You know those *Doctor Who* Post-it notes I got you? Can you flag the pages that are set in the hospital for me?'

I wanted to get some insight into how she perceived things had gone down. It was a good visit, and before my excitement waned and I tired too much, Elizabeth's mother arrived with the babysitter to pick her up.

When they had all left, Beth and I sank into our big orange sofa. 'You'd better take your blood pressure,' she said.

I slid the cuff over my right bicep, and rested my lower arm on the armrest. I took three deep breaths and pressed the button on my home blood pressure monitor. 171/112mmHg. That wasn't good.

After lying together in the dark for a while – no funny stuff – we decided that it was best to distract me from my perseveration. Tomorrow would be a new day, and while Beth went across the street to do a yoga class, I was to take on A Big Project. Sorting out winter clothes, random clothing rearrangement and screwing a fancy modern-design hook to the wall for hanging scarves. There were to be no falls or driving screws through my hand. Resurrection was one thing, but we had to draw a line.

Going into any new task, I was finding that one of the hardest things was modulating my expectations. Walking to Methodist Hospital from 15th Street? No problem. Manoeuvring along a single row of seats to see the Brooklyn Nets play at the Barclays Center? Utterly nerve-wracking.

On top of that, my self-perception was a mess. A couple of months post-stroke, I had already normalised the time when I was still clearly broken, and any task completed was a clear triumph. In my head full of pink goo, I thought that I was coming to resemble Ricky Brown again, and tasks that couldn't be completed in the style of pre-stroke Ricky felt like defeats.

Beth knew better though, and before she headed across the road to the YMCA the following afternoon, she talked me through the project again. I kind of got it by the third go-through, and after she left, I ran through it in my head again, and got started.

The initial problem was simply getting my body into position to organise the stuff that needed organisation. The refrain of October – 'Why is there always something hard pressing against my left side in an agonising fashion?' – had now been replaced by 'Why is everything always below waist level?' All the adjustments I had been making to compensate for my weak left leg, including weeks of hyperextending that knee, had left my body complaining about bending over and crouching. I had even been moved to raise this with Ranjan. His response was encouraging: the hyperextension should ease off, he said, when my leg muscles were stronger, and moving to outpatient rehab in Midtown where they had weight machines and the like would probably help with that.

Nonetheless, the clothes sorting was tortuous until, eventually, I had done what I could, and I moved on to hook hanging. I didn't make this easy for myself, but instead followed my usual routine, utilising spirit levels, support plugs, electric drills, a pencil and so on. This went swimmingly, although holding a pencil, a screw and a plug in my claw-like left hand simultaneously did lead to a couple of drops. All in all, I didn't feel too bad. I was using a power tool like I was a grown man, damnit!

I still had to admit that I had spent the evening working at the limits of my organisational, physical and anxietal limits. Anxietal wasn't even a word, to boot. I was glad when time came for me to press 'send' on the Chinese food order Beth had set up on her computer before she left, and settled down to await her return. I was a little bit emotionally on-edge. However, when Beth got home, she was able to calm me in short order: I had done a good job, look how far I had come, etc.

When we had got ourselves together, we watched the James Bond movie *Skyfall*, which had been on our list of things to do for a while. After my *You Only Live Twice* Thanksgiving shower, I was in the mood for some Bond. It was good, but not the *best Bond ever* I'd been led to expect by the reviews. Then the film took an interesting turn.

Beth was the first one to be affected by the sight of Glen Coe, in all its terrible, haunted beauty. Once she was off, however, I was away too, as I realised how close I'd come to never seeing the beautiful country of my birth again. Yes, my lights would have switched off too quickly for me to even be aware of the loss. But, y'know, *Scotland, man.* It was good to be alive, and have Glencoe, Calton Hill and the Moray coast.

Because, you know what? Everything was below waist level, but everything was OK.

15

Never Enough

At least, that's how things seemed at the end of November. By the time we spent Christmas Day at Paul and Jen's, everything felt a little different. Like many stroke survivors, I was still grappling with emotional lability or, as it's also charmingly known, emotional incontinence. It was still hard to shake the dark thoughts that clustered in my mind, but from the inside, this seemed entirely reasonable.

Whenever Beth ran an errand and I was left to my own devices, I couldn't stop thinking that the day when her sense of obligation to her disabled boyfriend would run out must have been approaching. In my mind, the endless work she had done since the night of The Event suddenly wasn't evidence of the strength of Our Thing. It was, rather, filling a finite bucket of love that must surely have to be emptied sooner or later. Then what would I do? Trying to find a new job in the post-financial crisis world had been bad enough when I could – I thought – pull an endless succession of all-nighters and close billion-dollar deals. Without Beth's help, I would be left to run through my savings in short order and sit at home mourning my latest and worst loss.

Jen reminded me that feeling down at this time of year was far from unusual.

'I mean, it's not like for you guys,' she said, 'but I feel like we've had a pretty hard end to the year. The holiday season is stressful enough – we've been scrambling around, dealing with deadlines, over-scheduled evenings and weekends, extra shopping – but now Mom and Dad aren't doing so great. There was the hurricane, of course.

'Then there was Sandy Hook.'

On the morning of Friday, 14th December, a young man in Connecticut had killed his mother at their home before driving to Sandy Hook Elementary School and shooting twenty six- and seven-year-old pupils and six more adults, then turning the gun on himself. Although Jill's school in Brooklyn had been really good with the kids, Jen was struggling with it.

'Everyone's struggling with it,' she continued. 'Here in the metropolitan area, people are already disproportionately stressed about their personal health and job stability.'

Tell me about it, I thought.

When Beth was home, things weren't so bad. She knew the things to say to calm me, and her voice was as soothing as ever. We would sit together and watch holiday television. Easy-going stuff, like those list shows of *Twenty Best Things of a Thing Ever* that they show on BBC America.

One evening, we tuned into a programme called *The Brit List*. This particular episode listed the *20 Sexiest* Brits.

'You know,' Beth said, 'I like skinny British men in their middle age—'

'I've told you, we're calling it the Early Clooneys!'

'Whatever. Have you noticed that they've had to fill this out with a car? And a candy bar!'

Certainly, we were beginning to feel our way into a new normal. For the moment, Beth was working from home. I would spend the mornings working through a battery of simple exercises and tasks around the flat before preparing lunch, doing the dishes and setting to work on some random computer project that would take infinitely longer than anticipated – on this particular day, it had been trying to get a telephone calling card to Scotland. Then it was time for a quick walk to the pharmacy. Beth chummed me along as we tried to get a refund to account for not having had her insurance card with us when we first picked up my latest prescription. The weather was unseasonably balmy, the sun was out, and – bonus – I was feeling steady enough to pick up my stick and hold hands as we strolled through the Windsor Terrace neighbourhood of Brooklyn, just across the Park Slope border. Beth didn't have her debit card with her, so they couldn't issue the refund, but we had a nice old time regardless, chatting not unlike the way we always had on the balcony or on the fire escape stairs at her old apartment in Crown Heights.

When we got back to the flat, the nursing service had changed tactics. Now, the ambush was combined with a pincer attack. After a long wait, my visiting speech therapist was finally ready and approved to visit, and my occupational therapist was also ready for her latest pop-in. They were both trying to schedule a visit for the same time, naturally. I suggested they put their heads together, so I didn't have to do something dangerous, like swallow and put out a grease fire at the same time. Speech won. The speech therapist turned up in the late-afternoon.

What is it with speech therapists? I wondered. They're all lovely. It must be some sort of quantity theory of niceness. Or maybe at the dawn of time, they nicked all the humanity from the occupational therapists.

Beth headed back to work, and Mary – a jolly woman in early middle age – suggested that we begin with a reading test. She asked me to pick a book at random from the bookshelf. That wasn't wholly advisable, so I slid past *Trainspotting* and Alasdair Gray, and James Kelman's Booker-winning swearfest to Chris Brookmyre's *Quite Ugly One Morning*.

'That looks interesting,' Mary said. 'Can you read me the first page?'

'Are you sure about that?' I asked, and pointed out the opening words: 'Jesus Fuck.'

We managed to find a passage that was a little more PG-rated, and I skipped through a page or so to Mary's satisfaction. When that was done, she looked around and identified the toys overhead as *Doctor Who* memorabilia. William, Patrick, Jon, Tom, Peter, Colin, Sylvester, Paul, Christopher, David and Matt were all lined up around a scaled TARDIS that hovered on a shelf above the big orange couch.

I decided that I liked Mary.

'Well, I don't think you're experiencing any difficulties with your speech.' She smiled kindly when I finally paused for breath, about thirty minutes into an exhaustive monologue regarding the intricacies of the continuity of the show (1963–89, 1996 and 2005–12). I had passed my speech and memory evaluation, even if I had forgotten to remind her to call in to the office at the time she asked.

'The VNS is really just concerned that patients can function at home,' Mary told me. Pleased to welcome the world back into the flat, I could go beyond that and talk the hind legs off any poor soul that cared to swing by Monahan-Brown Towers.

I'd gotten the hang of the walking stick, too, and Beth and I would take short walks with no particular destination in mind. These walks were pleasant – we could chat easily as the novelty of being outside together on a crisp New York winter's day distracted us from weightier issues. Then, building on the pharmacy visit, our expeditions began to have goals. One pleasant Friday afternoon between Christmas and New Year, we struck off towards Methodist Hospital for me to get an angiography. It was a ten-minute walk, so we budgeted for forty.

Since Beth had first told me about her visit to the aneurysm awareness group, we had made it to a meeting together and I had discovered from my fellow attendees that suffering a ruptured aneurysm is quite similar to going through a haemorrhagic stroke. It tended to involve getting wheeled into an ER, unresponsive, late on a weekend evening, with potentially catastrophic results. Generally, it was something best avoided.

Doctor Ayad had explained that it was best to get as much good information about my aneurysms as possible. How big were they? Were they smooth or knobbly? Where were they, exactly? So he had signed me up for this angiography, an imaging of the blood vessels in my brain.

As Beth and I walked and shuffled along, respectively, the tree-lined avenues of Park Slope suggested a classical Elysium dropped into a Victorian patchwork of stoops, bay windows and finials. I was a tested hero, selected by the gods to be rewarded with a blessed and happy life among Pindar's splendid trees, borne along by Plutarch's soft winds. Or something.

Then we arrived at Methodist, and I was plunged back into the stroke patient's Kafkaesque world. This time, I didn't register the gentle, considerate ramp that catered to the patients and the Park Slope. This time, the main entrance looked like a scene from M.C. Escher's *Relativity*, with stairs and pathways entering and disappearing from my field of vision at random. It was all very airy and modern. Eventually we found the *bi-plane intervention area* indicated by the appointment letter which, disappointingly, did not have a Sopwith Camel hanging from the ceiling.

After not too long a wait, we were called into a small examination room. I was quite happy that, as a little blood was taken, just the right amount spattered across the cold, speckled grey linoleum floor to appear dramatic crime-sceney, but not enough to swim in. Job done, the nurse departed, and after Beth and I had had a chance to sit together for a bit, I was wheeled into a low-key operating room.

In his usual, calming fashion, Dr Ayad explained that the contrast dye I was being injected with would cause a warming sensation, like I had wet myself.

'You might experience some minor discomfort, as we begin the procedure,' he continued. 'That's usual.'

He didn't mention that there's a scene in *The Exorcist* in which Regan MacNeil gets a carotid (or neck) angiogram, and according to director William Friedkin, this angiography sequence was the scene in the film most likely to upset audiences.

Entertainingly, The Cure's 'Never Enough' pulsated through the OR as my procedure proceeded. I thought to myself, 'Why not throw on Joy Division's desolate "Unknown Pleasures" to really get us all in the mood?' My amusement was doubled when I looked up the lyrics afterwards. Someone in Methodist Hospital had a wicked sense of humour, because the chorus of 'Never Enough' kind of described my procedure. Go on, look them up. I'll wait . . .

While Robert Smith moaned away, the miniaturised equivalent of a camera on the end of a pipe cleaner was pushed into an incision in my groin and through a passage of blood vessels up into my brain. Now, I would encourage everyone to take any angiogram that is recommended to them, since it's not horrible and you'll feel fine a day later. It was about as comfortable as that sounds, though. Groin-wise, at least. The other warning Dr Ayad had given me before the examination was about the hard, marbled-sized bit of scar tissue that would be left just above my groin. On the plus side, that would dissipate soon enough, and the drugs – Valium and Versed – were pretty good, to the extent that there was little remaining nausea when everything was done.

Appropriately, given the soundtrack, the results turned out to be like a grey, British shower: depressing or reassuring, depending on your mood. The best-case scenario would have been a single aneurysm, treatable by coiling. The fact of my two aneurysms was confirmed, but in the short time since the work-ups that had been performed in the aftermath of my stroke, they had remained stable and relatively small. The initial diagnosis, though, was that coiling was out, because the aneurysms were situated at junctions of blood vessels, and the wire mesh and any associated stent might have blocked the flow of blood. The hope was that we could approach them with a watching brief and treat them by clipping at an applicable juncture. This approach had its advantages: first, it would prevent blood from entering into the aneurysm sac at all, so that it could no longer pose a risk for bleeding; and, second, it would cause the aneurysm to shrink and scar down permanently after the clipping.

On the other hand, it would still be brain surgery, with all the attendant risks. Still being in recovery mode, I wasn't ready for that yet.

In attending our aneurysm awareness meetings, Beth and I discovered that each of the survivors of a brain haemorrhage has a story about his or her experience that has been practiced many times. Each catalogue of disaster had been turned into a sort of narrative. I suppose that a kind of Brechtian distancing effect is needed in order for the survivors to be able to discuss the events and results of a brain haemorrhage. Otherwise, it's all a bit, 'Yeah, so after they removed the catheter, I started learning how to walk again . . .' That's borderline depressing.

On the other hand, one of the haemorrhage survivors was keen to find out if she could somehow rebuild accurate memories of her haemorrhage and its near aftermath

Dr Ayad expressed some surprise at this. 'How many of you would actually want to remember what happened?'

All the blood and shit and piss and fear and uncertainty and pain?

'I would,' one of the group replied.

Dr Ayad looked around the room, and the raised hands indicated a roughly two-to-one split in favour of knowing.

'There seems to be a gender divide,' he noted. The men in the room were relatively incurious in this regard. The women, as well as myself, wanted a clearer recollection of what had happened to them. There was, it seemed to me, a way to do this. If you talk about The Incident and The Aftermath often enough and with enough people who were there, the repeated details build something akin to a memory. It's like that childhood recollection where you're not sure if you actually remember the experience, or just the details practiced in telling the story or hearing your parents repeat it. In any event, it did seem that the aneurysts wanted an understanding of what had happened to them. They had a very human desire for meaning behind the inexplicable. After all, what was the point of having a catastrophic brain haemorrhage if you weren't going to take something from it?

I decided to start attending a creative writing workshop a short distance north of Park Slope, in the back of a bookshop-cum-art gallery-cum-gift shop in Boerum Hill called Grumpy Bert. Like me, like everyone, the woman who led it was a different person to the one she was born as. In her case, when she was an infant, she had been flown from South Korea to Philadelphia to be adopted by her white, single, American mother.

The workshop was comfortable and supportive and smelled of hazelnut coffee and brownies. It was filled with a small group of people trying to find their writing and themselves. When we were set twenty minutes to write, I began writing the origin story of the guy who died and came back to life beginning on a rainy day in Flushing Meadows, Queens.

It had been a strange last quarter of the year, and there was still Hogmanay to get through. Since New Year's Eve was traditionally the biggest holiday of the year in Scotland, it was the time that I missed home the most. The Celtic emotion would burst from a facade of Aberdeen-sourced granite and I would weep for Glencoe and my family and friends and my late mother and grandfather, and all that I'd left behind. Yet for all the tears that had been spilled recently, it was hard not to approach this quiet New Year, seen in in our little apartment, as the gift that the root of the word Hogmanay would suggest. As Ryan Seacrest on the telly counted us down to the dropping of the Waterford Crystal time ball in Times Square, Beth and I rose from the sofa and held our champagne glasses and each other.

'Happy New Year, Baby. Thanks for everything. I love you. You're the love of my life.'

'I love you. Happy New Year. We got through it!'

It was a new year and a new life, and I was feeling . . . good?

My brain watched itself for a second. Yes. Good.

As we entered the new year, life began to take on a less institutional rhythm, as Beth continued to work from home, fitting in short walks around the neighbourhood with me. Physical therapists and visiting nurses and faltering attempts to figure out the story of what had happened since the end of September kept me out of her hair while she did her work.

Finally, after the worries about the numbness in my left eye, I made it to the optician around the corner. I was concerned about how things would go. Would the stroke have wreaked unnoticed havoc with that eye? Would the capillaries at the back of the eye have burst, or narrowed or thickened as a result of years of high blood pressure?

The doctor did that test involving the pupil-dilating drops, then checked out the capillaries with the magnifying lenses in one of those ophthalmoscopes they use to look at the structures behind the pupil. It's a good test, because this is where these small blood vessels can be viewed and often any problems here are likely to be repeated in small blood vessels in places in the body that can't be seen, such as in the kidneys. Fortunately, the test didn't show up anything bad, and my prescription was largely unchanged from my previous check-up some time during the Mesozoic era.

After these sorts of little unsupervised trips, and now that I had made it out to a couple of workshops, Beth and I became more ambitious. I put on a tie and a now loose-fitting suit, and returned to Grumpy Bert to share a few words on the subject of being 'Lost' together with twenty other workshop participants. I talked about how, four months previously, I had lost my youth, my job, my short-term memory, the ability to walk and the feeling on my left-hand side. I was learning to build my own narrative of what had happened to me.

Soon after this, Beth and I headed out to JFK airport for a flight to Los Angeles. It hadn't been so long ago that we were sitting in HJD discussing whether we should cancel our flights and reservations to the annual *Doctor Who* convention that we had been to in each of the previous two years. By the time we were ready to set off for LA, I was unreservedly looking forward to it, and to catching up with friends.

It turned out, however, to be a very New York departure. Getting out to JFK by public transport wasn't the quickest thing, and we missed our initial flight. In the rush, I even managed to leave my laptop at security. Good for the folks at the airline and in security, though: they got it back to me as soon as I noticed it was missing.

The flight itself was sold out and filled with airplane clichés. The seat right next to me was filled, and more, by a huge fella. My left side complained whenever he brushed against me. Of course, there was a baby nearby who screamed the whole way from New York to LA. When I peeled myself from my seat at the end of the flight, I could understand why Beth's mother had asked whether I was approved to take a cross-country flight.

In the end, though, it was all worth it. We got to see old friends and meet new ones. The discussion panels were good, too. But recovery is not a smooth story. I was exhausted when we got home, and Beth became concerned that, shortly after falling asleep at night and waking up in the mornings, I was having fits. For some weeks, I had occasionally been feeling a tension in my left leg, and if I flexed in the right way, I could generate a good old shake. A coughing fit would generate a similar response in my left arm. Although Beth was familiar with the leg and arm shake, these night-time fits were still quite disturbing.

Over four months after my stroke, I was still experiencing new symptoms. I would also feel tingling sensations sometimes in my left arm and, occasionally, leg. These seemed to be good signs that sensation was returning.

One day, back in Brooklyn, we ventured out to visit Paul and Jen without the aid of a car service, but it was hard going. Towards the beginning of the trip, I was breathless. When we arrived at the Waterfront District, I was quietly gasping for breath, trying not to make too much fuss. You would think I would have learned my lesson. We got through lunch and the beginning of a pleasant afternoon, but eventually we had to cut the visit short and order a cab.

When we got home, I lay on the big orange sofa and tried to relax.

'Take deep breaths, Honey,' Beth insisted. 'You control it. Don't let it control you.'

I tried to reply, but my lungs were wooden, rheumatic and stiff, only allowing one word to escape at a time. Seven weeks of superhuman effort, and here we were again.

I wanted to be OK. I didn't want to die again. I wanted to stay here with Beth's warm, life-giving hand on my chest. I didn't want this to be the rest of my life.

'I . . .' I gasped. '. . . think . . .'

Another few gasps, then another word. '. . . we . . .'

Soon, I lost track of how far through the sentence we were. I spat out the next two words quickly, breathlessly: '. . . need to . . .'

Jesus. How long was this going to take? I tried to fill my empty, collapsing chest with enough air to get out another word.

'. . . call . . .'

Not an ambulance, this time. Another car service took us the eight blocks to my home from home at Methodist Hospital. Neal met us there. Beth didn't need to manage this situation entirely alone.

This was the emergency room where I had been admitted on the night of The Event. As on that night, some of the less urgent cases were sitting in a waiting area, greyly waiting to be called. Doctors and nurses and paramedics quietly moved among gurneys.

While we were being admitted, Beth said the magic words, 'He's short of breath. He thinks he's having an asthma attack.'

Sparky had told us before that the secret to getting quick service in an ER, if you couldn't fake a good – or preferably, really awful – cerebral haemorrhage, was to claim an asthma attack.

But I was, in fact, having an asthma attack. I was allocated one of the gurneys, and a resident doctor quickly arrived and introduced herself.

'Hello. I'm Doctor Athena Mihailos. What seems to be the problem?'

Everyone was introduced, the symptoms were described and confirmed, and Athena strode off to source a round of drugs and a nebuliser so I could breathe them into my lungs as a mist. After it had all arrived and I was breathing more easily, the sense of throbbing red panic diminished and Neal and Beth and I began to have a grand old time. We waited for delivery of a further prescription for various types of steroids and began to speculate about whether we would be home in time for *Doctor Who*, of course.

I removed the mouthpiece to join in for a second. 'Athena. What a great name.'

'Yeah, who is that?' Neal wondered. 'The goddess of knowledge?'

'I think she's the goddess of war,' Beth offered.

Speaking of the goddess, the doctor arrived with the steroids. Neal decided to put the question to rest. 'Can you tell us,' he asked Doctor Mihailos, 'is Athena the goddess of war, or the goddess of wisdom?'

'Both,' she growled, and we all laughed and got to chatting.

Athena hadn't immediately recognised the young woman accompanying the guy suffering the asthma attack, but after a quick reminder of my now-legendary bleed, it all came flooding back to the young doctor with the long, dark hair who had seemed so serious at the beginning of October. She and Beth began discussing the subject of telling family members that a loved one was on the way out.

'I remember you were really upset.'

'I felt like you guys were trying to tell me that he was probably dead.'

'Well, yeah . . . But there's always a chance that they might not die, so . . .'

So, the effort to keep me alive continued. When I'd last had my meds tweaked, I had been taken off Lisinopril, my original blood pressure-reducing ACE inhibitor, because it was causing a regular, dry cough. I had been put on Labetalol, a beta blocker, instead.

I was always wary of beta blockers. They reminded me of Big Bill Werbeniuk, and how they'd finished his snooker-playing career. The 250lb Canadian drank around six pints of lager before a match and then another pint for each frame he played. Apparently, he did this to counteract a tremor in his arm. Whatever it did for his tremor, all this booze put a terrible strain on his heart, so he started taking Inderal. This beta blocker was considered to be a performance-enhancing drug by the World Professional Billiards and Snooker Association, so he was fined and suspended. Big Bill went home to Vancouver to live with his mother, on disability benefits. He played cards, watched telly, went bankrupt and died of heart failure.

On this day, the outcome wasn't nearly as bad for me, but we found out that Labetalol did have the risk of causing bronchial spasms, and was not advised for asthma patients. Which was a shame, because it was keeping my blood pressure under excellent control. Instead, Athena sent us home with a new rescue inhaler, a steroid inhaler, and orders to visit the doctor treating my hypertension. We settled into the big orange couch again, and Beth and I began our latest effort to lead a somewhat normal life.

16

Sisyphus

Life seemed to have become an endless procession of trips to the emergency room, punctuated by more regular check-ups. The week before Christmas, I had written an impassioned message to a friend regarding the reluctance of a family friend of hers to address his high blood pressure. The gist of it was, that was fine for the family member, but they needed to think about the devastation they'd be wreaking on their loved ones when the pigeons came home to roost.

Shortly after I had finished with my correspondence, I got a call to schedule my latest late-breaking home nurse check-in. Not for any particular therapy this time, but for the nurse to check my vitals. This included taking a blood pressure reading, which was a bit high on the first reading on my right arm. Then on my left arm. On my right arm again. By the time we took a follow-up reading with an electronic monitor, we'd been on the phone to Doctor Im, and I was very stressed out. Another high reading. The recommendation from the nurse and Doctor Im was that I get myself to the emergency room or an urgent care centre so that a doctor could see me in person, and fiddle with my meds as necessary.

My feeling was, my readings had been good for the past month, so why were we getting me stressed on account of one set of bad readings? My frustration with this aspect of the evening was getting me even more het up. However, the professionals were concerned enough to make a big deal about it, and in light of my recent email, it would have been ridiculous not to get things checked out.

Beth and I walked to the urgent care centre on Fifth Avenue. I'd never been to one of these places before, and it all seemed pretty great. You could get seen right away. The interior design was decent quality, in a non-committal, abstract, modern style. Outside, Park Slope Urgent Care Center happily presented a glass frontage to Brooklyn's Fifth Avenue. The restrooms hadn't been painted with blood, shit and snotters, like in the average ER. In a regular hospital, the emergency room was where people would go when they didn't have or couldn't afford medical insurance. Where they go when they can't put the visit off any longer. The absence of screaming in the urgent care centre was also encouraging, as was the doctor, who had an excellent manner and was the first professional that night not to totally freak me out. She tweaked my meds in consultation with Doctor Im, got me some referrals for cardiologists, and by the time a car had taken us up back up the Slope again, I felt a lot calmer.

Then I realised that, in a classic stroke patient move, I had left my phone in the car. Even then, the nice lady who had replaced me in the back seat picked up my call, and 30 minutes later, the driver was back with my spare brain. The one that remembered the dates and times of my scheduled appointments and my correspondence and almost everything else I had to remember. After a disheartening interlude, we had managed our way through another tricky situation, and I felt encouraged.

Talk of depression had been commonplace in my journey as a stroke survivor, from the Irishman with the aneurysm to the woman with aphasia, to the repeated warnings to look out for it from my doctors around the time of my discharge from hospital. Post-stroke depression is a horribly common condition, and up to a half of stroke survivors suffer from it. I had read that its prevalence peaks six months after a stroke.

The position of the lesions on my brain seemed to subject me to greater risk of post-stroke depression, but my relative functionality was a positive. PSD is linked to a high level of stroke-related limitations and disabilities in functioning, especially in performing what my doctors called 'activities of daily living'. These ranged from being able to wash and clean myself to being able to manage money and transport myself within the community. The basic ADLs were within my capabilities, particularly with the grab bars that were spaced around the bathroom. Nevertheless, I did seem to be at some risk at this stage. In addition to my lesions being on an area of the brain called the basal ganglia, after the leaps and bounds of the progress I had made in the early days of rehab, post-discharge advances were necessarily more incremental. In order to stay encouraged, it became important to, firstly, recognise smaller advances and not to take new achievements for granted, and secondly, not be discouraged by expected set-backs. One day, Beth sanctioned a solo trip for me to deposit a cheque. During my trip, I noted that I could independently take a multiple-step journey (including a subway ride) to a previously unvisited location, even if it was only a couple of stops to a familiar neighbourhood, and then transact my business upon my arrival, step up onto the curb without giving a second thought to the positioning of my left foot, and get up the subway stairs without absolutely clinging onto the bannister for dear life. These little things gave me a sense of achievement and encouragement for the day.

On another day, I might have ruefully reflected that, as Albert Camus had written of Sisyphus, my scorn of the gods, my hatred of death and my passion for life had won me nothing but 'that unspeakable penalty in which the whole being was exerted toward accomplishing nothing'.

Soon after that day I deposited the cheque, I headed off to my first Young Stroke Survivors Support Group meeting at the Rusk Ambulatory Care Center in Midtown, which wasn't far from my ugly, old, unsuited for purpose office building. Beth came, too, and kept me right on my instructions for getting there and back, so this was less of an independent activity. I still managed to misjudge how long it would take me to get to her office, leaving us late for the meeting, then lost my phone again during the course of the expedition. These events left me disconsolate, even though, in the recent scheme of things, they needn't have been the end of the world. The problem was that I was now far enough along the road to recovery that part of me wanted to immediately make the jump to fully functional. Anything less was a disappointment. That was unreasonable of course, and in any event, it ignored the fact that the vast majority of us, even the able-boded, are dysfunctional to some degree. Thankfully, Beth was able to pull me out of my funk with that observation and other kind remarks.

'Also, think about it.' She smiled. 'That's exactly the sort of thing you would have screwed up before your stroke. It'll turn up.'

The Young Stroke Survivors Support Group was also a great help in giving me a boost. I'd encourage any young stroke survivor to attend these kinds of meetings because I found out that there are two types of stroke survivor, and to turn Alexei Sayle's remark about there being 'two types of jazz and they're both crap' on its head, both of these sorts of people were great. There were the folks who were doing better than me, and they were inspirational, and there were those who weren't quite so well off but doing their best, and they were pretty inspirational, too – if not more so. Maybe Camus was right, and the struggle itself towards the heights is enough to fill a man's heart: that, as he pushes his huge rock up the steep hill knowing it will roll away before the task is complete, as it always must, one must imagine Sisyphus happy.

We kept working on making my incremental gains. The visiting therapists' visits continued, and on the days they didn't come, I did my exercises assiduously. Grasping onto the back of a chair, I would stand against the bathroom door and bend my knees and let my back slide down the door before pushing back up again. I would lie on the bed and imagine a thread running from the ceiling to my belly button, and pulling me up into a bridge. Beth would fill a large yoghurt tub with lentils and a paper clip and a couple of dimes and an eraser and a plastic token and a short screw and a little luggage key and a tiddlywink and a spring; I would root around in it with my numb left hand and try to find them. The little key was always the hardest.

It all paid off when the therapists from the visiting nurse service came to the conclusion that I was ready to begin outpatient therapy at the Ambulatory Care Centre. Actually, it was an intimidating thought. My application for the city's paratransit service had been approved, but none of my medical advisers particularly advised using it. The disabled around the city were picked up in whatever order made most sense and were dropped off according to the same system. The amount of time it would take to get anywhere depended on where the service needed to make pick-ups and drop-offs between where the bus was, where you were and where you were going. Even if my executive function was good enough for me to be organised to get to the rehabilitation centre in time, I was still going to be spending endless time perseverating and waiting for minibuses in the apartment, at the centre, on the street. At this point in his recovery, this stroke survivor needed certainty in his life and not too much idle time on his hands. So before Beth returned to work full-time, we took some practice rides on the subway. It wasn't too bad, and I learned some interesting stuff about my new limitations as we walked into the 15th Street-Prospect Park station.

'You know what the worst thing is?' I asked Beth.

'Something hard on your left side? Things below waist level? Things above shoulder height?'

There were a lot of worst things about suffering a stroke.

'No. I can handle stairs now, kind of, and flat surfaces are fine, but slight inclines are the worst. It's the foot drop. I mean, I really concentrate on stairs so that's not a problem, but I'm never ready for inclines to be difficult.'

Nevertheless, I decided that I was going to take the subway to my rehab appointments, even though my experience of taking the subway from Brooklyn to Midtown for ten years for work was that that was bad enough without having to freak out every time someone – or something – touched my left side.

Beth previewed my route to Manhattan with me at the weekends, and we noted on my phone – Beth's old one, after the one that I had lost on our visit to the Young Stroke Survivors Support Group had not, in fact, turned up – the numbers of the trains I would take, the names of the stations where I would change to avoid a mile-long walk at the far end of my journey and where I would get off, and the numbers of stops between them. Before long, I was able to make the trip into Manhattan on my own. My appointments were outside of rush hour and, clinging on to the handrail – but not for dear life – I was able to negotiate the stairs down to the platform and back up again. The route quickly became familiar as it unfolded.

When I emerged from Grand Central Station for my first appointment, I had managed to stick my way up and down stairs, change at the right station, get on the right train and get off again at the right place. I stood outside a quiet exit after rush hour had abated and spun my phone around in my hand to make sure I was setting off in the right direction. Eventually, I figured it out and made it to the ACC, proud as anything.

My latest physical therapist, Carrie, met me in the waiting area and directed me to complete a lengthy history and intake form, then escorted me into a long gym lined with treadmills facing out of windows, racks of multicoloured hand weights and one of those little wooden staircases to nowhere. Even a trampoline!

After Carrie had done some measurements to check how my movements on my left side had been limited, she showed me some stretching exercises to extend the reach of my left arm, holding my upper arm out at a right angle, placing my forearm, perpendicular to that, against a door frame, and leaning forward. Pushing against the tight resistance was oddly satisfying. Then she set me to work walking on a treadmill, and quickly identified the foot drop issue. When we sat down on a couple of the little desk chairs dotted around the room, she reminded me to concentrate on planting my left heel down first.

'But I think you've got a lot of upside. Tell me, what would you like to concentrate on?'

'Well,' I told her, 'my girlfriend and I live in Park Slope, and when I was in hospital, we would talk about how we wanted to be able to go running in the park together. I'd like to do that. I'd like to be able to kick a soccer ball with my daughter. Long-term, I'd like to get back to where I was before the stroke.'

'That's a great attitude. I think we can do that, if you're conscientious about coming to all your sessions and doing your exercises.'

The following week, Beth and I returned to the ACC for another battery of tests, and my psychological intake evaluation. Setting up and checking in for the appointment was an exercise in occupational therapy in itself. After getting through the process, I was disorientated, anxious and generally functionally impaired. The day before I had got the appointment, I had received a call indicating that I should report an hour early for intake. Given that I'd gone through an extensive intake and check-in procedure at the same location for that first outpatient physical therapy appointment a week earlier, and had even registered for the fancy palm-scan check-in that they used, I wasn't sure if this would be necessary. After calling every number associated with the psychology department that I could muster, I was none the wiser, since nobody picked up at any of the numbers. I left a message on the morning of my 2p.m. appointment, but nobody called back. I checked into the psychology department, and did my fancy palm-scan check-in, but nobody made any enquiry about intake documents. In fact, it didn't come up until, just as I was comfortable that there were no problems, my doctor came to collect me for my appointment and asked the receptionist for my non-existent documentation.

So, the receptionist and I went back down to the ground floor and picked up the requisite papers and questionnaires, and I sat in the waiting area filling them in with a whole bunch of the same answers that I'd previously filled in for the physical therapy intake, together with some additional information with more of a slant towards neuropsychology. Once again, the information required was very detailed and, to a large extent, related to the facts surrounding my stroke, and the ensuing hospital stays.

I turned to the receptionist and remarked, 'Well, at least nothing's happened during that period to screw with my short-term memory, eh?'

Eventually, the supervising doctor decided that we would have to press on with the examination and interview part of the intake, so the balance of the paperwork would have to wait.

The examination parts of the session felt like they went OK. Counting down in leaps, identifying words and images, matching images with letters, remembering numbers and reciting them back in a different, requested, order, were all fine, except the last one was a little tricky when enough numbers were loaded on. I did manage to screw up one of the old HJD favourites, though. I knew who the president was, and the year, the month and the date. The day, though? After spending it up to that point navigating the intake procedures and going through a long, detailed informational interview – and not having a job to go to – I had no idea whatsoever.

Nevertheless, the interview portion of the appointment was pleasant enough. My doctor seemed capable, informed and business-like. What was not to like about an extensive psychotherapy-style interview? It was the closest I had come to being the subject of a feature interview in a music magazine, and as if I was a British indie star of the late twentieth century, the conversation did turn to the subject of alcohol use. We discussed it at such length that I wondered if it was something to do with my accent again. Not only had I not said anything to indicate a craving for beautiful, tasty booze, I didn't even drink that much in the wake of my stroke.

The doctor felt the need to clarify something. 'I'm not a teetotaller or a temperance advocate,' she said. 'It's just that with the associated risks, especially for a stroke patient, we have to be sure that you're aware of them.'

All in all, it was an educational meeting, and I got some interesting hand-outs regarding brain injuries. Perhaps most interesting was the one on right- and left-brain injuries. Beth had expressed the opinion that a having a right-brain, left-sided stroke may have been more fortunate for me than the opposite outcome, since I had been so left-side dominant that I wasn't likely to succumb to left-side neglect or inattention to the left side of the body. The part of my hand-outs describing the effects of injuries to different sides of the brain listed something called 'left neglect' as a deficit resulting from a right-side brain injury. It didn't list 'right neglect' as an injury resulting from a left-side brain injury. I could only guess that this was a result of our society's bias against the left-handed among us.

In our wrap up, I learned some interesting big-picture stuff from the psychologist that I either hadn't known previously or that hadn't been expressly laid out for me before.

'I agree with you and your girlfriend. You shouldn't even be thinking about returning to any type of work until you've completed your rehab at Rusk. If you go back to work earlier, you'll be at risk of utilising coping strategies that are likely to be disadvantageous to your long-term recovery. If you've been referred to Rusk, you've had a serious injury. You'd benefit from attending weekly rehabilitation sessions and, again, working would interfere with your rehabilitation needs. I would recommend that you start psychological rehabilitation, and I'm going to set the wheels in motion for you to attend weekly individual psychotherapy sessions. Hopefully, those should start in February.' She made some notes.

'What should we do in the meantime?' I asked.

'Just keep doing what you're doing, and don't overdo it.'

She then went on to tell me that when a patient has made an encouraging recovery, and is used to operating at a high level of functionality, other folks may be less likely to notice their deficits. That's why, according to the Brain Injury Association of New York State, education of the individual with a brain injury, their family, employer, case manager and others is extremely important. If the individual, family, employer and others do not understand the injury and its effects, inappropriate treatment may follow. So I had been referred for a full bank of neuropsychological tests, and ongoing appointments in the psychology department.

In the meantime, I kept doing what I was doing, and as the weeks of physical therapy passed, Carrie had to delve deeper into her bag of PT exercises and get a bit creative to extend the anticipated limits of my physical upside. After jumping, two-footed, over a line taped on the gym floor, I progressed to jumping over small objects.

'Great! Now, have you got your phone? Cool. Do you consider yourself a New Yorker? We're New Yorkers, right?'

'Yeah. I fold my pizza before I eat it. I've watched a guy squeeze a bottle of mayonnaise all over a subway seat, and be so crazy that he didn't even hang out at the other end of the carriage to see people's reaction. I'm not proud to admit it, but I've picked up an egg salad sandwich I've dropped on the Queens Plaza subway platform. It was a really good sandwich.'

'Wow. That's a soft filling! You *are* a New Yorker.' She paused, and tapped away on her phone. 'OK, I'm gonna send you a text. You've got to be able to walk and text if you're a New Yorker, right?'

I walked along the wooden flooring that ran around the gym, reading Carrie's message and glancing up and tapping in and glancing up and not walking into someone and sending a reply and feeling pretty good about things.

In time, my physical therapy session was scheduled to allow me to come straight from a visit with Ilana, my psychological therapist. She was a senior psychologist at Rusk and had a few years' extra life experience on me, too. I felt I could talk to her, which I suppose was the point. There was no stereotypical couch; we sat across from each other at her large wooden desk and talked. Early on, after she had gleaned my own impressions of my deficits, she recapped and enlarged on some of the results of that initial neuropsychological intake evaluation.

'It reflects the same sort of things you describe. Some people might not appreciate the difficulties you're experiencing because of your premorbid level of education and professional attainment, but the way these tests work, they can establish from, say, your vocabulary, what your baseline pre-stroke performance might have been.'

'Oh, that's cool,' I remarked. It was. That struck me as really clever.

'So, as well as the significant reduction in your processing speed, you're experiencing what we call increased attentional variability, which negatively impacts your memory. Are you familiar with the DSM?'

I was, kind of. 'I've heard of it. It's some sort of desktop reference for mental health, isn't it?' Beth is fascinated by it, and has always wanted a copy for herself. My friend and helper and lover, who, without knowing it, had been preparing for so long for that moment when her vocation would reveal itself.

'That's right. It's the *Diagnostic and Statistical Manual of Mental Disorders*. It's a publication of the American Psychiatric Association, and we use it to diagnose and classify mental conditions. In addition to those cognitive changes, the reduction in processing speed and the attention issues, you've been diagnosed with the DSM IV diagnosis of adjustment disorder with anxiety. This diagnosis isn't unusual for individuals who have been through a life-changing traumatic event.'

She paused while I absorbed this new information.

'Well, that certainly adds up,' I smiled, wryly.

'If you agree, I think that our treatment goals should include building awareness, understanding and acceptance of the changes in emotional and cognitive functioning that you've experienced as a result of your stroke?'

'That sounds good. Thanks.'

Then Doctor Grunwald gave me a piece of advice that I wished I'd received ten years earlier, and that I've carried with me ever since: 'Recovery from a stroke is a lengthy process,' she said. 'It's not unusual for it to take two years or more for someone to reach the upper limits of their recovery. So it's good that you're aware of the changes that you've experienced and that you're working hard to change the things you can. There may be other things you have to accept.

'You know, when I was going through school to get my PhD, I was going through a difficult period. I was having problems with my mother and the work was difficult, and I came across this thought experiment that I've found very helpful. If you're experiencing a problem in life, and finding it hard to get past, visualise your life in two years' time and see how the problem looks then. If it's not a problem any more, don't worry about it too much. If it is, well, then you're going to have to do something about it.'

I enjoyed my weekly visits with Doctor Grunwald and my thrice-weekly physical therapy sessions. My intake evaluation had been right. Rehabilitation is a full-time job. One evening after Beth got home from work, we sat in front of the telly, discussing the events of that day and the previous day. There were large chunks I couldn't remember. With the help of the calendar on my phone, I was able to say where I'd been, and when. However, if you'd asked me to describe any of those places? I would have had no idea. I had been increasing the amount of stuff I was doing, and I could hardly believe how quickly I had maxed out into exhaustion, forgetfulness and clumsiness.

'But, you know,' I thought to myself, 'I'm kinda messed up. It is what it is. Maybe things will be better in two years.'

Fortunately, the next day was a day off for me. Beth's alarm rang at the usual time, and she headed off to the Financial District with a reminder to me to get up and shower, do my exercises and get some minor chores done. The next thing I knew, there was somebody at the door.

Beth walked in. 'I knew I'd find you in bed. Did you get my texts?'

I rolled over in bed and reached for my phone. Over two hours had passed. The first missed text read, 'I've just been laid off. Coming home now.'

17

Disability and Benefits

It seemed as if every time our love story cleared a hurdle, another impossible challenge would spring up in front of Beth and me. Just a short while before she lost her job, I had made a list of *30 Things I Can Do Today That I Couldn't Do Until Relatively Recently*. Like a researcher working for a programme listing twenty sexy Brits for an American audience, I had had to stretch a bit.

1. Walk down stairs without hanging on to the banister for dear life.
2. Ride a stationary hand bike.
3. Have the foggiest idea what a stationary hand bike is.
4. Walk to Methodist Hospital in less than an hour.
5. Kneel down.
6. Get cereal off the top of the kitchen cabinets.
7. Knock up a delicious dinner for two without swearing one fuck of a lot.
8. A comedic soft shoe shuffle (with the emphasis on *comedic*).
9. Arm curl a canister of flour.
10. Towel myself down with some degree of vigour.
11. Brush my teeth by moving my left hand, and not my head.
12. Get up in the morning.
13. Sign my signature without too much discomfort (though just as illegibly as before The Event).

14. Turn my left hand palm up.
15. Go a couple of hours without bursting into tears.
16. Throw in a football (that hurts).
17. Reset the water heater in less than half-an-hour.
18. Take my blood pressure without feeling depressed.
19. Take two Labetalol high blood pressure pills without suffering a fainting fit.
20. Spontaneously think about breaking into a jog. Before realising that's not going to happen, obviously.
21. Stay up a little late.
22. Walk without hyperextending my knee.
23. Use a hospital toilet without getting nostalgic for the 'Pull for help' cord.
24. Not perseverate.
25. Not perseverate.
26. Not perseverate.
27. Not perseverate.
28. Not perseverate.
29. Not perseverate.
30. Not perseverate.

By the time we had done a post mortem on the events of the morning, I had realised that I was going to have to delete numbers 12 and 21 from the list and add another couple of *Not perseverate*s. I felt pretty bad about that.

The shortest possible period after which it was tolerable to terminate an employee returning to full-time work after their partner had suffered a near-fatal injury had elapsed, and Beth had been made to suffer that cruel Financial District fate where you're called into a meeting and told to bring your essential items with you. Because when the meeting is done, obviously, you'll be escorted to the main door and anything you've left behind will be sent to you at the earliest opportunity. As the scene unfolded, Beth was numb and just needed someone to tell her things were going to be OK.

Her love had saved me, in the most literal sense. I had been strolling in my grandfather's garden, considering the state of my face, and feeling very tired. Somewhere in the background, there was an inkling of how hard it was going to be to dig myself out of the grave and get fixed. I was ready to rest. Then, in my blood-soaked mind's eye, I had a vision of Beth. I remember seeing her smile, and, most strikingly, her eye. Her left eye, specifically. I've described her eyes as hazel, but really they are brown around the pupil, and then a grey-ish colour as you approach the edge of the iris. The brown looks as if it generates its own light, and never more so than in that moment. The vision was so vivid that I sometimes wonder if I had regained consciousness for a few seconds, even though I know I didn't. Regardless, I knew in that moment that I had to come back. I wasn't even sure that I would be able to come back to stay, but I had to tell my girlfriend that I had loved her, loved her still, and that everything was going to be OK. Or that she'd be OK, at least. I didn't get to do that in the moment, but the thought got me close enough to the shore that she, with the help of the EMTs and Doctor Ayad, was able to drag me back to the land of the living.

As Beth, who'd been my rock for these past months and longer, made her way home from being sacked, I was sleeping a deep and dreamless sleep.

What made things even worse was that we would no longer be able to make the so-called COBRA payments to my health insurer that had enabled me to continue my health insurance coverage and avoid having to pay the million-dollar sticker price for saving my life, keeping me alive and continuing my rehabilitation regime. We accelerated our efforts to secure disability benefits for me, and began to look into securing food stamps.

The initial online application for disability benefit was designed in such a way that this cognitively challenged guy needed more than three attempts to complete it. I had heard word of a severely hemiplegic patient who had had an initial application rejected.

After that, I was also required to submit a written submission and attend a follow-up interview to fill in the stuff the Social Security Administration had still missed. The mailing address for certain material I had to submit was that of the New York state offices in the state capital, Albany. With a zip code in the state of Kentucky.

The whole process seemed hopeless and crazy. My favourite part was receiving yet another letter simply informing me that a failure to turn up for an appointment to submit my material could result in a dismissal of my case. No mention of an appointment itself, or a time or place; no request for any further materials.

When your confidence in your mental state is already shot, receipt of such a letter can really fuck with you.

Eventually, we found out that the final submission of my claim was to be made at the Social Security office in Brooklyn. When Beth and I arrived for the appointment, it was as if we had stepped into an episode of that show *The Americans*, where the KGB sleepers settle near Washington DC. Not in the sense that the state had arranged for a spy to be waiting at the offices to offer us sexual favours, but in the sense that, although I was living in the US, I felt like I had a good understanding of what it was like in the Soviet Union of the eighties. The facade of the social security office was the embodiment of classic Urban Brutalism, and the length of the early-morning line outside suggested that we were all queuing for bread. The rush into the building when it opened and the old ladies in headscarves having screaming rows with the security staff backed that up, too. I didn't think Stalinists would have tolerated the stink of piss in the elevators, though.

The woman who collected my materials and submitted them for evaluation at the state office was nice enough. Ilana had already told me, though, that no one was successful with their first application, and we would have to appeal to have any hope of getting anything.

When Paul and Jen found out about the latest developments in our lives, they took us out to the farm for the weekend. Even given what had recently occurred, the rolling, green countryside was relaxing. Or as relaxing as it could be in the circumstances. We talked, we ate, we read. We strolled through the local, open shopping mall. There was a light rain, almost a Scottish smirr, hanging in the air. It wasn't that bothersome, other than it felt peculiar on my left cheekbone, which made me sad.

By the time we got home from our visit with our friends, Beth had run the numbers and the scenarios. Sitting at the dinner table, she told me that with no income except, possibly, at some undetermined point in the future, disability benefits, and the COBRA payments and the New York rents and the utility bills and my unemployability and the continuing sluggishness of the financial employment market and her total exhaustion, we were going to have to do something, and quickly.

'Do you remember,' she asked, 'when we first started dating, you said that you'd only planned to come to the States for a couple of years?'

'Yeah. That escalated quickly.'

'And how we always thought that at some point, we'd move to Scotland, but there didn't seem to be any way for us to get there? Now there's no way for us to stay here.'

As soon as she said it out loud, there was no decision to be made. It had been made for us.

The next day, we called my father to ask if we could stay with him for a bit.

'It won't be for long,' I told him. 'Just long enough for us to suss things out and get on our feet. We'll pull our weight. Do stuff around the house.'

I hardly even knew how to ask. Just a few short months ago, I'd insensibly held an imaginary phone to my ear in my hospital bed and sobbed to my father who wasn't there, 'I'm sorry. Oh god, I'm so, so sorry.'

Sorry that I hadn't been home more often. Sorry that I hadn't called more often. Sorry that I hadn't written more letters. Sorry that I hadn't seen Mum one more time. Sorry that I'd almost gone and died without saying goodbye. Just, sorry. So, so sorry.

That day, he said to me, 'Of course you can stay. If you can't rely on family, who can you rely on?'

I should have wept then.

Now the decision was real, and we had a finite amount of time to make it all happen, the weary young woman and her broken beau. Thankfully, we didn't even realise that it was impossible. We just kept doing the next thing.

We started applying for an unmarried partner visa. At our initial meeting in another sleek Midtown office, our immigration lawyer outlined the hoops we would need to jump through, like evidencing two years of cohabitation and the genuineness of our relationship. Evidence that, if you've never had to prove these things, you wouldn't think to gather. How do you write the thing that keeps you up in a little hospital waiting room with a short, two-seat, faux leather sofa and keeps you going and going and going and going?

In March, our first application was refused. We gathered more joint bills and got letters from museums and galleries setting forth our family memberships and letters from my doctors. Most of all, we got letters of support from our friends. We got one from Paul and Jen. We got one from Kirk and his wife Andrea. We got one from Cole. We got one from Beth's old flatmate Mat. We provided each of them with a suggested form, and they each asked if they could make changes to the letters, add embellishments, personalise them. Jonathan asked if he could just go ahead and rewrite his.

As I am sure has been disclosed to you, he wrote, *last year, my friend Richard suffered an untimely stroke. It is not an understatement to say that this was a life-changing event – and I would be remiss to not say that I feared for my friend's life. Beth was by his side through it all. Whenever I was there but she was not present, he would ask me when she would be returning. His life had changed, and in a perverse twist, while much in his life was clouded and confused, his most critical survival requirements were crystal clear to him – he needed Beth. I watched as she stayed by his side as their lives literally changed overnight. She didn't waver, or falter: she personified what it means to be a partner. Her life was with him, whatever the circumstances, and in the early days after the stroke, those days seemed grim. But stay she did, and thrive because of that he did.*

As the process dragged on, we continued to put one foot in front of the other. Finally, I received another ominous letter setting the appointment for me to submit myself to the physical and mental examinations required as part of my evaluation for disability benefit. When we went along that spring day, after a morning session at the ACC in Midtown, we found that the exams took place in a different building to Brooklyn's Social Security Administration asylum. This was a building more like something from the work of M.C. Escher, but darker than the lobby at Methodist Hospital. The walls weren't quite at right angles to each other. The floors were slippy enough to foil attempts to use a walking stick, and were slightly cambered at random intervals. To add to the feeling of Bedlam, there was a nice long wait between the mental and physical exams, during which I listened to a fellow applicant rant at length about her waiting time at a volume clearly intended to draw someone else into her solo conversation. All while another applicant stood in the corridor spitting out random letters. Or, as the doctors might have termed it, 'taking a sight test.'

I was reminded of one of the old arguments deployed for stripping people of their benefits: don't treat the disabled like they're disabled, or they're going to act all disabled. Sure enough, I was feeling pretty non-functional by the time I had completed my physical examination, and was finally called for my mental evaluation. The final Orwellian irony of the process was that this was taking place four months after I had started the application, and six months after my stroke. I couldn't see how my performance today could be relevant to the amount of work I would have been able to do in November. Or December. Or January. Or . . . Well, you get the drift.

Beth was allowed to sit with me as I was subjected to the test. It followed a pattern I was used to now. We related my medical history, then I completed tasks like naming the objects depicted in pictures that were shown to me. The examiner asked me questions about a passage that he had read to me. I copied a diagram that I was shown. I named as many animals in a minute as I could. All that sort of thing. The examining doctor asked me to remember another list of three objects, just like Ali used to do back at HJD.

'Can you tell me what that the three objects were?' he asked a couple of minutes later.

'An apple, a ball and a penny,' I replied.

'Thank you. Now, remember those objects. I'll be asking you what they were again, a little later.'

This is too easy, I thought. I couldn't throw this if I tried.

I was asked to draw a series of clocks showing particular times on a series of pre-drawn circles. Finally, we came to the end of the tests.

'Now, can you tell me again the list of three objects I told you earlier in the examination?'

'Rug. Clock. Flower.'

Beth turned to me after the examination was complete to whisper, 'That was a bit much. There's no way he's going to fall for that.'

In fact, I hadn't just deliberately flunked the exam. Still, my answer was what Elizabeth would call an 'epic fail', and explained the look of utter befuddlement on the examiner's face when I delivered my answer with an air of complete confidence and conviction.

I had remembered the words *apple*, *ball* and *penny*, as *rug*, *clock* and *flower* for a reasonable reason. They were the objects that I'd been asked to remember at the Ambulatory Care Center that morning.

It seemed my time in New York and with the medical teams at the Rusk Institute and Methodist Hospital was coming to an end. Still, they hadn't been able to establish what it was that made me so susceptible to my haemorrhagic stroke.

After a very pleasant Friday lunch on a pretty, early summer's day at a local Italian restaurant with Matt From The Darts Team, Beth and I sauntered over to our home from home at Methodist Hospital so I could get fitted up for an ambulatory EEG that would measure voltage fluctuations within the neurons of my brain as I went about my business over the weekend. It was always a strange sort of pleasure to return to Methodist, because everyone was very nice, and I had little memory of my original stay. I could build a sense of that narrative that the members of the aneurysm awareness group and the Grumpy Bert workshop were trying to build. We walked along the quiet, residential side of the hospital, and Beth was able to point out my old window and mention that view from the step-down unit that was pretty, and wasted on me.

As always, I was struck by the look of the lobby when we arrived. As the novelty had worn off, I had found that it wasn't so much that I liked the lobby, but that I liked that the person who'd designed it seemed to have had a blast. After all this time, explorations of infinity and architecture be damned, Beth was a whizz at finding her way around Methodist, so we promptly rolled into the epilepsy unit for my appointment. We were invited into a treatment room by a technician, Isabella, and the process of my latest cyber-conversion began with a head measurement.

As Isabella reeled off various numbers (60 . . . 60 . . . 36 . . .) while carefully measuring from the bridge of my nose to the ridge at the back of the top of my skull, from ear to ear, and so on, I made one of the cracks I always made about the size of my huge, Scottish head. Like the wee kid with the massive heid from *So I Married an Axe Murderer*.

'I'm an inverse Weeble. When I fall down, I can't get up.'

'It's perfect,' she demurred, and I briefly conjured fantasies of the numbers describing some kind of perfectly proportioned Vitruvian skull that would leave men and women all over the borough swooning. Beth was chuckling in the corner though, and I realised that Isabella simply meant that I was, somehow, the right size and shape for the EEG wires. God knows how, given that the folks at the Motorcycle Safety School set me up with an XXL helmet when we were learning how to ride that little pink scooter.

The process continued, with what felt like various guide marks being scribbled on my head, and the application of the adhesive and the sensors. At this point, there was some discussion regarding the opening of the window. The adhesive was stinky, like nail polish remover, but as a child of 1980s Scotland, I was all for advocating that the window be closed tight and any cracks stuffed with towels. To no avail.

Eventually, twenty wires leading from my head were sticking into the little receiver box that I would be carrying around night and day until Monday. I was told to close my eyes while I was subjected to bright flashing lights, to check that the receiver was registering whatever fluctuations resulted. I don't know the exact degree to which the EEG reflects what is going on in the brain, but at this point, mine was screaming, 'Make some *fahking noise!*' and imagining an Orbital gig somewhere in a field off of the M25.

When we were done, I was carrying the receiver in a jaunty wee purpose-made shoulder bag and the sensors were covered by a woolly beanie that I hoped marked me out on that summery weekend as a Brooklyn hipster rather than a neurology patient. The bandage that covered the sensors and collected the wires into a bundle poked out of the bottom of the hat and ran down my back like the Predator's tendrils. Like the Drop Foot System at the HJD, all this gear plugged into my interest in sci-fi body horror. We were told not to let the apparatus get wet. As well as that, I wasn't allowed to chew gum through the duration of the test. Apparently if I did this, that's all the EEG would capture for the duration of that activity.

Thereafter, it was a fairly normal weekend. Rain was forecast, so we lounged around at home in this strange interlude, watching telly and footering around with preparations to leave the country.

As we reached the end of the experiment, I had to say that the set-up was quite literally nipping ma heid. Not to forget that adhesive! On day one, I had noticed a nasty pain behind my right ear that turned out to be a broken little blister that the adhesive had caused. So I was glad that I hadn't huffed too much of the stuff.

When we returned after the weekend was over, I was hoping that the attending technician would be able to tell me what I thought about the fact that I had spent a substantial portion of the weekend watching all six hours of a miniseries about the Hatfield and McCoy families feuding on the Kentucky-West Virginia border in the late nineteenth century. Maybe because of a pig. It wasn't entirely clear, but I felt pretty sure that my blurriness wasn't solely attributable to my stroke. If the moral was that all this feuding and killing was pointless, then what did that say about watching all this feuding and killing?

In the end, the return trip to Methodist was pretty frustrating. For starters, I was beginning to find that my visits to Methodist generally seemed to leave me feeling a bit gimpier, I guessed that this was something to do with somehow returning to the inpatient mindset. It didn't help that this was a grey, dreich day. In fact, on this particular Monday morning, the rain was lashing down. As I angled my crappy street vendor brolly against the wind and positioned the receiver box with the twenty wires sticking out of it under my jacket, I felt like one of those kids who takes an egg home from school with orders not to break it for a couple of days.

Things continued downhill from there. I was in possession of coffee vouchers to be cashed in at Methodist that had been bequeathed to us by Matt From The Darts Team. Amazingly, although I had come to understand that Methodist's cafeteria usually closed between 8a.m. and 11.30a.m., from 11.30a.m. to 5.45p.m., and again from 6p.m. to 7.59a.m., it was open just before my appointment was scheduled. Like a good stroke patient, I happily strolled in and set about finding myself a decaffeinated beverage. It turned out that there was no decaf in the hospital with an Institute for Cardiology and Cardiac Surgery! I decided to take my life in my hands and redeemed my voucher regardless.

By the time I found the epilepsy unit again, I'd had quite enough irritation for one day. Then I was called in to begin the removal process. Well. Have you ever visited the dentist for a teeth cleaning, and had the hygienist put their foot up on the arm of the chair so they can really get some leverage on the scaler?

The technician indicated that I should close my eyes, because she was about to apply the 'water solution'. I'm clear on what water is, but as I understand it, a solution is a homogeneous mixture of two or more substances. We didn't get into a discussion about what the other one or more substances that were going to melt my eyeballs might have been.

Apart from a visit to the dental hygienist, the other wonderful experience I was reminded of was having some cheap barber in the New Town of Edinburgh cut my hair as a kid. And by cut my hair, I mean grab onto tufts of hair with his blunt scissors and pull them out. Now, just as then, it didn't seem judicious to tell my tormentor what a shitty job she was doing, so I followed the old approach of jerking in pain and taking sharp intakes of breath.

This didn't really work, and I ended up with a hole in my head. Needless to say, I needed another hole in my head like I needed a . . . Well, you get the idea.

Why this happened, I'm not exactly sure. It may be that I've got a very mild case of my late mother's allergy to non-precious metals. Maybe it was a reaction to the adhesive. Or, most likely, it was a reaction to having an electrode amateurishly torn off my forehead.

Oh, and the Hatfields and the McCoys? Well, I can tell you that when the families were on *Family Feud* in 1979, they competed for cash prizes and a live pig that was kept on stage during the games. It's complicated, but the McCoys kind of won.

The results of the EEG didn't reveal anything of interest.

Beth and I handed in our notice to end our lease of the flat on 15th Street. We sold or gave away anything that was too big to ship to Edinburgh. We arranged to ship the possessions that we hadn't disposed of. We gave little one-eyed Cyclops to Ex-Flatmate Mat and his wife Jenni, because she got on with their cat Noah and because she had the softest fur and because she fulfilled the contract whereby you gave her food and water and shelter and in return she loved you and because she was the best cat.

I met with Elizabeth's mother to discuss how best we could maintain my relationship with my daughter: by my keeping up regular contact, making it clear that our move was in no way a reflection on how I felt about her but something that had arisen from circumstance, and talking with her directly

192

about all this as openly and honestly as a grown-up could. I met with Elizabeth herself the next day, and a local coffee shop served as neutral ground. Our relationship had been faltering as I remained a boring, stroke-y daddy.

It didn't go great. I ran through the talking points I had discussed with Linda, and tried to keep Ilana Grunwald's injunction to remember that Elizabeth, although a smart kid, was still only ten years old, and I was a man in his late thirties. When I delivered the news of Beth's and my forthcoming move, Elizabeth wobbled for a second and excused herself to go to the women's toilet. I thought it would be best to give her space, and considered my coffee cup and waited.

And waited.

Some more time passed, and a text came in from Linda. Elizabeth had texted her from the toilets to ask her to come by from around the corner and take her home. It was all too much to deal with.

I knew how she felt. Being a grown-up sucked. Nevertheless, Beth and I kept putting one foot in front of the other, because that's what grown-ups do.

We found out that it would cost as much to take those feline jerks Seamus and Geronimo to Scotland as it would cost to send over all of our possessions, and we had them chipped and certified for travel by the US Department of Agriculture and arranged to take them anyway. They probably hadn't even noticed my absence while I had been an inpatient at Methodist and HJD. They had been present throughout Beth's distress, though, and we would have missed them.

We applied for a visitor's visa for Beth to come to the UK so that we could be together while we waited for her partner visa to be processed, and so everything would be totally above board. We moved out of the apartment on 15th Street and moved in with Jen, Paul and Jill while we crossed as many 't's and dotted as many 'i's as we could. When we were moving out of our flat, the cable company tried to screw us out of our deposit on our shitty cable box, of course, because that's what the cable company does. The building's superintendent told us that a number of items we had left in the flat for safekeeping on the day we were moving out had been put out on the sidewalk. We didn't see them there, but when we told the super we were going to call the police for some help with that, our possessions were miraculously found.

As we took our last walks around Brooklyn, near Jen and Paul's place, that Red Hook summer felt hotter and more humid than previous summers in the city, and that summer smell of hot trash smelled hotter and trashier. New York was in my blood forever, but I wasn't the New Yorker who would pick up an egg salad sandwich off a Queens subway platform any more. We loved New York, but for now, we were tired and it was bringing us down. Our hearts had already moved as we bought our tickets to fly to Edinburgh. We had a last night out with our old buddies from Harry Boland's, and then we started off on a new adventure.

Two hundred million years ago, I had read, Scotland had been a desert. Then I had left forever. Right enough, as we flew above the banks of the Forth, my old home was no more. Friends and family had moved on, Mum and Hugh were gone, and even though I recognised my old dad, he was a different man now. On the edge of this new old world, I held Beth's hand, and I was scared. Over sixteen years, I had traversed the old new world, and by the time I was through, my friends and family were an entirely new group of people. I had changed, too – my sandstone heart broken, yet held together now by succulent American oak. As I surveyed this new land, I had strength. Beth had brought me back from Buckie, and, my Charon, she had sailed me safely across the Styx so I returned from the underworld alive even though I had no coin for her, and owed her everything.

Scotland as I had known it was gone, but this new country was going to be our adventure together.

18

Valhalla

The connection at Heathrow had been tight, and we took a taxi into Edinburgh without the cats. At my father's house, I got off the phone with the airline representative and relayed the story to Beth.

'She says that they missed their connection. Which makes sense – have you ever seen a cat trying to read a departure board in an airport? They're rubbish!'

'Right? And pulling rolling luggage with no thumbs?'

'Exactly. Anyway, they can't get them on another flight today, so they're going to keep them in London over the weekend. The animal handling centre in Edinburgh is closed until Monday. But she tells me that the centre at Heathrow is really good. They'll have loads of room to move around, much more than in Edinburgh, and they have lots of handlers to look after them.'

We reassured ourselves that Seamus and Geronimo would be fine and that it hadn't been selfish to haul them across the world with us, by picturing them making the most of a free weekend in London, checking out the changing of the guard and taking selfies by the London Eye. They arrived in Edinburgh after the weekend was through, and this latest version of our little family began to make itself at home.

We borrowed a book of Edinburgh city walks from the local library, to help Beth learn the city, and me help re-learn its rhythms and routes. With Beth in tow, I found myself taking unexpected, meandering detours that unveiled new views, as well as more obvious, expository routes.

Our timing had been good. During our February trip the previous year, twilight had begun to fall before 5p.m. and many of Edinburgh's landmarks had kept restricted hours. We'd been concerned about the weather that the Scots complain about like a persistent drizzle, but during our last days in New York, the increasing heat and humidity had begun to take its annual toll while reminding us of the symmetrical yearly trudge through snowbound sidewalks before stepping confidently off a curb into filthy, black, freezing slush up to the knees.

To my amazement and in contrast to my memory, Edinburgh, on the same latitude as Minsk, turned out to be temperate. Shortly after our arrival, my father's newspaper screamed the headline SCOTS SIZZLE IN 86°F HEAT-WAVE! We were tickled by the incongruous use of Fahrenheit in a British newspaper to increase the sense of sensation, the red font that the paper had used to pick out the impossibly high number, and the fact that year's highest temperature in New York City had scraped 38°C, or 100°F.

We joined a running group that jogged gently through Princes Street Gardens on Saturday mornings. One Saturday, as we passed the Ross Fountain in the shadow of the Castle, the leader of the group commented on another spell of unusual weather.

Beth's response seemed to me to sum up the capital's climate. 'Yeah, what the hell is this? It's raining, but it's not raining!'

As the days waxed and waned, we took advantage of this interval in our lives. One day, we took out our book of walks and decided to follow a route that would lead us to Calton Hill.

Walking east along Princes Street, the gothic rocket ship of the Scott Monument didn't look as tall as it had back in the day. It did have a heft that I didn't remember, though. From there, Scotland's National Monument on top of the hill looked like it should have been all the way down in Leith. Like its spiritual successor, the tram, it only got as far as the East End. Our route took us through the Old Calton Burial Ground, which Abraham Lincoln benevolently surveyed from a plinth. His monument marked the graves of a small number of Scots who had died in the Civil War, all on the Union side.

Uncertain of the details of the journey after a long absence, I repeatedly took my phone out of my pocket to check our progress. Edinburgh had always claimed to be on seven hills, like Rome. Arthur's Seat, Blackford Hill, Braid Hills, Castle Rock, Corstorphine Hill, Craiglockhart Hill and the one we were on now. Or maybe it was the seven in the old rhyme:

> Abbey, Calton, Castle grand,
> Southward see St Leonards stand,
> St Johns and Sciennes as two are given,
> And Multrees makes seven.

Or maybe the map in my pocket was right, and Edinburgh was really built on countless hills and under innumerable bridges, a labyrinthine rat run. Whatever, now the Nelson Monument loomed above, so I took a chance on my gut. 'This feels right. This way!'

Because going with my gut had always worked before.

We headed up a narrow, stone, tree-lined set of stairs signposted as Jacob's Ladder.

Re-emerging into the light, we oriented ourselves again. Horatio's telescope still stood on its end to the north reaching to 561 feet above sea level, but a little closer now. Peering deep into Edinburgh's heart. We crossed Calton Road and set off up another flight of stone steps to the summit. Halfway up, a monk in grey robes and Reeboks stopped us with an expectant smile. He passed me a little plastic amulet bearing an exhortation to WORK SMOOTHLY for LIFETIME PEACE, and opened a small flip book to a picture of his temple. Then he passed me another little booklet and a pen, indicating that I could fill in my name, home country, a message of peace and a pledge. I fished in the pocket of my jeans for a pound coin, and the monk thanked me with another smile.

He indicated the little yellow flowers crowding into the stairway and told me in quiet, halting English, 'When the gorse is in bloom, it is the kissing time.'

I smiled back and nodded.

When we reached the top of the hill, we could smell the salty sea air blowing across the flat, open expanse of the park. Above, a plane sliced a contrail across the blue sky, having turned the shoulder of North Berwick.

That was always my favourite part of the flight back from New York, seeing the harbours of Leith and Newhaven laid out 5,000 feet below. Like the map I once poured across my parents' living room floor, tracing from where Mum fished me out of Newhaven harbour at low tide to where my father watched as I righted myself after capsizing under the Forth Rail Bridge. I never took that flight often enough. Not even after the desks at Cantor Fitzgerald, eighty floors above the desk of my ex-wife, had been turned to dust. Dust that had silted up the Hudson River, the Diamond Reef and the lungs of New York City's rescue workers.

Having taken a few breaths of recollection, I smiled at Beth and we started towards the top of the monument. Just a few steps into the 143 whitewashed stairs spiralling upward, the frame of a recessed window relayed the message, 'Almost there'.

'How brilliantly Edinburgh!' I exclaimed.

'It's still inside me,' I thought. 'Almost twenty years later.' Even now, when I took one of my little solo trips into town, I could feel the petrifying stoicism spreading outwards again to cold fingers and toes.

Closer to the top of the tower, another message in neat black paint exhorted us to 'Keep going on!' So we did. Of course. All the way to the thin door in time-travelling blue that, if we pushed it on one side and a stranger pulled on the other side, could be opened out onto a spectacular view over the National Monument, towards the Kingdom of Fife. In another direction, I could see that boutique hotel that looked out over North Bridge.

'Flexible thinking, Sonoko!' I thought. Maybe I didn't take criticism well because I knew what I was doing! Or maybe I had just been very fortunate. I put the old version of Ricky back in his box, and turned to look out over the Forth.

The ships in the firth contrasted with the boats of the new Scottish Parliament lying keels-upward in the shadow of the tower, wishing their architect's Mediterranean sun could dry them out. The ships out in the water were alive and productive, like the fishing boats Hugh's friends had sailed. I thought of him taking me to see Jimmy, who would lie on his waterbed in Seafield Hospital changing the channels on the television by blowing into an air pipe. The fisherman had broken his neck falling through an open hatch in the deck of his boat. The waterbed was to prevent bedsores, but Jimmy would let a fascinated wee boy hop up on it, too. Of course, I didn't see the tragedy at the time, only the excitement of the new, and the generous, garrulous fisherman. Now the boats just reminded me that Hugh and Jimmy were gone, as well as my mother. Back in Auld Reekie with my tail between my legs, taking this particular walk for the first time in in too long, it would take time for this to become a new version of home.

I brought my view back down to Edinburgh's Folly, the landmark we had really come to see. Scanning the National Monument from our telescopic eyrie, I tried to map for myself how the balance of Playfair and Cockerill's plans for the monument might have lain. Particularly the catacombs that were intended, two hundred years ago, to form Scotland's Valhalla, a place where the nation's heroes would have been put to rest. A place where Hugh might have been comfortable, after those wartime special operations in Albania and Malaysia. Not somewhere for a Scot who should have died three thousand miles away after a day spent eating fancy pizza, drinking, smoking and shagging.

I had no more success building the chambers in my mind that I had previously had picturing our old apartment on 15th Street, so we tumbled back down the narrow stairs of the tower to have a look from ground level. Down here, the monument's few pillars were overwhelming, and I was aware that it had acquired a power to move as a palimpsest that it could never have had in its complete state.

A caravan of Spanish tourists in bright anoraks was rolling down towards the road. As their laughter blew over Holyrood Park towards Duddingston Loch, and Beth wandered over to look at the Playfair Monument, it seemed I had been left with the place to myself. I sat on a low rock and rooted myself down into the land. Eyes closed, I imagined the grass spreading over my boots and pulling me in. When I opened my eyes again, I could see Beth heading back along the path towards me, the Doric columns behind me scattering sunlight around her. It was time to go home.

At the end of the summer, we headed to South Carolina for Beth's brother, Kevin's, wedding. When the celebrations were over, Beth stayed in Greenville and I returned to Edinburgh alone. Her partner visa application still hadn't been approved, and we had been advised that it was best for her to stay in the US for a bit while things were sorted out. It was a reminder of how the emigrant's – the well-to-do emigrant's – experience had changed since I made my original move to the US. We could continue daily video calls just as I did my weekly ones with Elizabeth, and we could regularly text each other. We kept each other up to date with what we'd been up to.

I told Beth how well NHS Scotland was taking care of me. My new GP had dismissed the key ingredient of the US-designed drug cocktail I had been taking to combat my high blood pressure as being a couple of generations out of date. Now I was taking just one set of pills once a day, with no sign of any side effects.

When I first checked in with her, the doctor told me that due to my stroke, I would have to take an assessment test before resuming driving. That was no biggie. We didn't have a car, and while I'd finally gained my NY licence not too long before the stroke, I had driven very little during the preceding decade. We had lived in New York City, after all. When I had taken my very first driving test in Edinburgh, so many years ago, it hadn't gone well. It had taken place not long after I had herniated that disc that had led to maraschino cherries and Oscar Wilde, and I had been uncomfortable and nervous in the lead-up to it. Suffice to say, the test was cut short after the examiner pulled on the handbrake and asked if I had been trying to get us both killed.

However, there tends to be a waiting list to sit the assessment test, so when a spot opened up I thought I'd better take it. I found myself back at the Astley Ainslie Hospital for the first time since a series of detailed neurological evaluations that had taken place shortly after we first arrived in the country.

The Astley Ainslie is an odd little city secret. It specialises in rehabilitation services for people who have suffered brain injuries, strokes, orthopaedic injuries, limb amputations and neurological disorders like multiple sclerosis. Unlike the Western General Hospital and the Royal Infirmary, our fellow Edinburghers didn't seem to be terribly familiar with it. Maybe this was because it was low-lying, and hid behind stone walls on all sides, spread across rolling grounds. Inside the walls, it felt like I had entered a time warp. As I made my way to the South-East Mobility and Rehabilitation Technology Centre, it was like roaming the grounds of an Edwardian sanitorium.

Then I was plunged even further back in time when I passed a building that, while of reasonably modern construction, presented a wooden gable end to the pathway, and a plaque declaring:

> Here stood the Chapel of St Roque
> who inspired many to succour
> victims of the Plague, 1506–1646

Finally, I reached the southernmost edge of the grounds. I took a seat on a bench, and called the DVLA. Revisiting the materials I had received about my assessment, I had found that in order to be allowed to sit the test I had to have informed the authorities of my condition. The guy who answered the phone asked a series of questions that I interpreted as intended to lead to a point at which he could reasonably advise whether I was fit to drive. However, he did indicate that a fuller questionnaire would be sent. In any event, an opportunity to regain a little driving confidence with a professional therapist and dual controls seemed like a good thing, so I moseyed on in.

Here, hiding behind another building as if embarrassed to disturb the time warp, sat the SMART Centre, all low-slung modern efficiency. When the clock struck eight thirty, they could check me in.

I wasn't what my assessor expected.

'The file says you're a solicitor. You don't look like a lawyer.'

'Thanks! I'm not.'

Soon enough, the assessment began. We ran through initial neurological and physical tests, before I was set up in a rig for peripheral vision and reaction testing, all computer-measured to determine whether I had passed or failed. Then, we would have a wee hurl around the grounds, and all being well, we would end with a drive around residential Edinburgh and the city bypass.

The therapist explained that the neurological testing would be less extensive than in my prior visits to Astley Ainslie. We were simply here to check that I was safe to drive. The testing was pretty low-intensity compared to what I had been through previously.

'Tap your finger each time I say the letter "A" among this list of random letters,' he began.

'Now, I want you to draw a copy of this two-dimensional representation of a cube.'

'How many words beginning with the letter "C" can you name in a minute?'

I set a new record for that last one. Or so he told me. Then we proceeded to the rig. It was totally steampunk. I strapped into a regular car seat, and Terry, the therapist, turned up the volume on the impossibly dated electronic 'vroom' noise that activated when you pressed the accelerator. Just above the faux dashboard was a big yellow light. I was to slam on the brakes each time it lit up.

Above that was an array of LEDs set into what looked like a repurposed garden sprinkler. Each time one of them lit up, I slammed on the brakes. That was the test for my peripheral vision.

Surrounding the big yellow light were two green lights and two red lights. More green than red light up? Hit the gas. More red than green? Hit the brakes again.

When I was done, the computer said I had passed, so we hopped into a Nissan Micra and tooled around the grounds until Terry was ready for us to cut loose. Fourteen miles and forty-five minutes later, we returned to the SMART Centre in one piece, and I felt a little less nervous at the wheel. As I made my way past the former site of St Roque's Chapel, checking my Edinburgh buses app to see when the 41 would roll up, I was amazed to reflect that a year had passed since that bank of neurological assessment tests I had taken to establish my eligibility for disability benefits.

It already felt like a lot longer, and it felt like a lot of things had changed for the better. Regardless, though, when I related the story to Beth after I got back to my father's house, she was still four thousand miles away. Our latest attempt to secure her re-entry to the country had included details of previous international trips we'd taken together, photos of us on those trips and pictures of us together at Kevin's wedding.

Then, at the end of November, our immigration lawyer asked if we could all get on the phone together.

'Thanks very much for getting on the call,' Anushka began. 'And Ricky, apologies for bothering you so late.'

'No problem. Nothing is more important than this. What's going on?'

'I just wanted to update you. I followed up on Beth's application today and was informed by a contact of ours in Sheffield that the caseworker is not entirely satisfied with your application, and has refused the application on that basis. We've not received any notification of this or any paperwork, so I'm anticipating that the decision is with a manager.'

We discussed what further materials might be assembled and remitted to the Home Office by the following day. We rustled up one final letter and sent it to Sheffield. I went to bed with no idea what we would do if this failed, then time stood still for three days.

Finally, another email arrived from Anushka.

'Ricky/Beth,' it read. 'Are you both available to speak now?'

We got on the line again.

'We've heard from our contact again,' Anushka said. 'The manager has reviewed the initial decision on your latest application for leave to enter the United Kingdom.'

'Anushka, you're a ham,' I thought to myself.

'Congratulations. It's been approved!' She sounded as delighted as we were. She had read all the letters from the friends and families and doctors, and seen all the pictures.

Exactly one month later, another Hogmanay was approaching. Another birthday, and the first anniversary of my stroke, had passed. It was a time for reflection. Back in New York, another stroke survivor friend liked to use Shabbat as a weekly milestone to gauge, and possibly adjust, his trajectory, noting that it was a bite-sized amount of time that lent itself to this kind of exercise. Passing from one calendar year to the next lent itself to a similar exercise, but taking a view of longer cycles. Having passed solstice, while dawn was staying at roughly the same time in Edinburgh, we were slowly digging out from absurdly early sunsets and taking the first steps towards the long evenings of summer. That is to say, we were emerging from the darkness.

Beth landed at Edinburgh Airport and walked past a big picture of Edinburgh Castle bearing the salutation 'Welcome Home' on Christmas morning, a year and three months after my stroke.

19

Jacobite Warriors

Over the next two and a bit years, Edinburgh did become home for both of us. Beth and I became fixtures at the pub quiz at the local bar, down the road from my father's home.

'Where are you from?' the locals asked.

'I'm from New York,' Beth told them.

'Why on earth would you move here from New York?'

She nodded in my direction. 'This guy. Also, are you kidding? I love it here.'

She interviewed for a job at a business that had just been taken over by an American company. The Chief Financial Officer asked her to tell him something interesting about herself, and she told him that she used to play in a competitive darts league in Brooklyn. It was the most interesting answer he'd heard all day, and she got the job.

Elizabeth and I maintained our weekly videos calls, and I spent some time with her in the States when Beth and I were able to make it across. She thrived, and I learned that, while Dr Grunwald was right about Elizabeth being a child and me being a grown-up, she felt more able to open up and talk when I shared some of the details of my new life with her. It wasn't always as boring to her as I would have assumed, I guess.

I went back to university and continued the perennial task of building a new Ricky. We travelled. Beth saw Mosstodloch in Moray where my family lived when my father worked in

Buckie. We went to Ireland, where she sat exams to be fully qualified as an accountant on this side of the Atlantic. We settled down in Stockbridge in Edinburgh because it reminded us of Park Slope, all coffee shops and charity shops and a bike store and an independent record shop. We spent a weekend tooling around Inverness and sailing along Loch Ness in the *Jacobite Warrior* to visit Urquhart Castle.

The next day, we took a walk along the lochside. The path was quite rugged, but this stroke bloke was coping well. At a quiet spot with a view across the loch to the other shore, I stopped to tie my shoelaces. Beth looked down, horrified. We had discussed why we were taking this trip up north; our experiences with the vagaries of immigration law and health-care law had pushed us towards what was about to happen, and in any event, it felt right now. Beth hadn't been thinking about that, though. We were sweaty, and there were midges everywhere, of course.

I had passed the test designed by Beth's former marriage counsellor, then therapist, then friend, some five years previously. Later on, during our balcony chats, we had agreed that neither of us was particularly interested in marrying again. The point wasn't to *have* to be together, but to *want* to be together, and it had turned out that we had wanted to be together. It had turned out that we had to be together.

On the bank of Loch Ness, Beth was aghast. 'Oh my god, Ricky. No. Not now!

'But yes. Of course, yes.'

That was how, just under a year later, we found ourselves standing in front of a small group of American expats, university classmates, pub quiz teammates and other friends in the South Queensferry Registrar's Office on the south shore of the Forth, with a view of the three bridges from three centuries that spanned the firth.

After saying a few words, the celebrant called forward our witnesses. Then, just as I had done in front of the jukebox at Harry's a month and a bit after that night on the bench, I went first.

'In the spirit of Our Thing, and before these friends and witnesses, these are my promises:

'To be grateful for, and to make the most of, this opportunity to be with you.

'To be open to spontaneity, and new experiences and adventures together.

'To keep making the choice to round you up to The One.

'To always try to help your life be better for sharing it with me.

'To always speak to you from the same room.'

I break that last one all the time, and Beth busts my balls for it every day.

Then it was Beth's turn:

'I promise to never give up on Our Thing, because we're keeping this.

'I promise to never stop making you laugh, because let's face it – the vast majority of my jokes are tailored for a very specific audience of one.

'I promise I will never stop encouraging you.

'I promise not to make any unilateral decisions. Also, I promise to support decisions that are important to you, even if it means you decide to turn down your honour from the Queen, and I don't get to go to Buckingham Palace.

'Finally, if you ever have a stroke, I promise not to let you cry.'

Finally, I could cry. When we were all done, two friends who were photographers took some shots. There's one of the two of us extending our ring fingers to the camera, and Beth with a big smile on her face.

She looks irreverent in that picture. Fucking classy.

I look like I'm the luckiest guy alive.

And I am lucky. And alive.

Beth asks from time to time, 'Do you ever think about your stroke? Are you aware of it?'

I think she's still a little surprised when I tell her that, yes, the residual deficiencies are always there. I'm always more or less aware of them, and particularly so when I'm tired. I have been very lucky, though: I'm fairly mobile, and given the location of my bleed, my expressive abilities are in good shape. Even the odd sensitivity that remains on my left side is weirdly enjoyable, in the right context.

The estimated five-year survival rate for haemorrhagic strokes is around a quarter. Among the survivors, only around a third of them will go on to live relatively normal lives, and even among that subset, survivors' experiences will diverge. Some of the luckiest ones will choose to ascribe the quality of their recovery to being stubborn buggers, and, sure, the competitive part of me that misses the intensity of my former life just a little bit and laughs when I pass some guy who is bellowing his putative importance down a mobile phone thinks that a competitive nature contributed to my recovery. Still, even that competitiveness is just part of the random set of variables that allowed for the sort of recovery I've been lucky enough to enjoy. I prefer to put much of the quality of that recovery down to the quality of the two and a half years I had already spent in Beth's company, and the crazy, ridiculous dream of trying to get back to them again. While at the same time, remembering that none of us lucky ones would be part of that lucky third without exactly that – pure, dumb luck. Someone being present at the moment of the brain attack, a major neighbourhood hospital with a specialisation in neuroscience, a quick ambulance, the exact location of the attack, any one of hundreds of more variables. If love and hard work solved all the problems arising from a brain bleed, there would be a lot more alive and happy people in the world.

Not that it was all luck. A lot of people did work really hard. The anonymous EMTs. Doctor Ayad, Doctor Im, Doctor Mihailos, Doctor Karp, Doctor Blum, Doctor Grunwald and Sparky and all the other doctors who attended to me. Steph and Sonoko and Liat and Michelle and Rodney and Ali and Dawn and Carrie and Ranjan and Mary and all the therapists. Paul and Jen and Jonathan and Matt From The Darts Team and Ex-Flatmate Mat and all the friends. Our parents, Ray and Kathy, and Paw Broon. Most of all, Beth, the love of my life.

In my post-stroke interest in the way the brain works, I've discovered that the latest theories indicate that the phenomenon whereby time seems to speed up as we get older isn't explained by the proportionality theory that suggests a year feels faster when you're older because that year is a smaller portion of your life. The psychology writer and broadcaster Claudia Hammond says that the phenomenon arises due to something called the reminiscence bump, which in turn arises from novelty. It's why we remember the experiences of our formative years so vividly; that's when we experience so many things for the first time. Sexual relationships, leaving home, first jobs. The details around them reinforce the formation of our identity. It's the reason your favourite album came out when you were seventeen.

People who undergo a major transformation of identity later in life tend to experience this phenomenon. I've certainly met other stroke survivors – who continue to cope with quite serious deficits – who appear to have been able to use that turning point in their lives to find new purpose and enthusiasms that keep them young-seeming. The lucky ones, that is.

I'm wondering if I should get remarried every five years – to Beth, of course – to slow down these remaining years and feel young. There's so much to fit in.

Epilogue

As Good a Place as Any

'Beth, honey. Do you think I should call the hospital?' I ask from the next room.

'You're breaking your vows!'

She's been putting it off, waiting to see how things develop. She doesn't want it to be nothing. However, we've been in that place before where the temptation is to delay, and the feeling is growing more intense. So Beth agrees that I should call Edinburgh's Royal Infirmary and try to convince them that they need to see my wife. The woman on the other end of the line asks for the details of what Beth is feeling, and I tell her everything I know.

'Can you give her the phone, please?'

'I'm not really sure that she's able to talk right now.'

'Bring me the phone!' Beth calls from the bedroom.

I do, and she makes it clear to the operator that we have to come in now. She's still a New Yorker, right enough. The hospital is on the other side of the city, so I grab the go bag and help my wife down the stairs to the car. It's a route we're familiar with, up and out of the lower part of the city where we live, through the city centre and off out past the edge of Liberton, where my father's father grew up. I've been ferried there with another asthma attack since we moved to Edinburgh, although that issue seems to have entirely settled down, now. I've had to take my father there a few times, and Beth and I have been there for any number of check-ups.

Not long after Beth is admitted, our friend Penny arrives. She's another American, an academic of a certain age, with whom we've become firm friends since moving to Edinburgh. She's Beth's kindred spirit, highly educated and feisty. For today, she's our Edinburgh Sparky – here to look after me as much as Beth, and help clean up the mess. Penny and I sit with Beth as members of the medical team come in and out. I suppose I must feel just about as helpless as Beth did on that night back in Brooklyn.

Penny and I chunter aimlessly on to try to distract Beth from any worries she might have, but things don't seem to be getting any better. Time passes, and the rotating cast of young women who have been looking after her are beginning to look concerned. It's beginning to look like there's going to have to be some sort of intervention. Penny can't stay.

'Do you want your partner to stay? Do you want to stay?'

'Yes,' we both reply, and I follow as Beth is moved to a bed that can be wheeled to the operating theatre.

When we arrive, I'm taken aside to scrub up appropriately, and when I return, the anaesthesiologist and the surgeon are talking Beth through what's happening.

'I like Irish people,' she tells the anaesthesiologist, and he does seem very assured and relaxed.

A nurse brings a chair for me and invites me to sit. As the procedure proceeds, I am instructed to stand from time to time while the chair is moved to where I am out of the way of the people who are doing the real work, and where I won't be exposed to anything that might be considered distressing, then I am invited to sit again.

There's a moment of quiet as everyone else in the room works intently, and for a second I fear the worst. Then, when the surgeon is sure that Beth and the baby are going to be fine, he asks if I would like to stand and see our son being delivered. Of course I would, and in no time our wee boy is handed to a couple of nurses and the four of us go into an adjoining room to put him under a heat lamp and massage some life into his little body and have me cut the cord that still connects him to the delivered placenta. Then we return to the theatre, where Beth has been made comfortable and can hold the baby for the first time.

It's all very efficient, and as I look around the wide, bright room and the expert surgeon and the anaesthesiologist and the nurses, and consider the midwives who had attended to Beth in the birthing centre, I think to myself that Edinburgh's Royal Infirmary is as good a place for Ruairidh Hugh Monahan Brown to be born as any.

Acknowledgments

I'm very grateful to the many people without whom I or this book – and in some cases, both – would not exist.

Thank you to everyone at Sandstone Press who gave *Stroke* a chance and helped make it something better than I could have imagined on my own. Thanks in particular to my sympathetic and insightful editor, Kay Farrell, who made the process of finishing *Stroke* fresh when that was exactly what it needed.

Almost everyone who appears in this book in one form or another deserves thanks, not least the legion of paramedics, doctors, nurses and therapists who walk the pages. Thank you to all of them, especially Dr Ayad and Dr Im. I hope that my affection for them all shines through this story. Thanks are also due to the many stroke survivors I have encountered on this journey, every one of whom is brilliant and brave in their own unique way. The same goes for their many supporters.

Thank you to everyone who took the time to visit me in hospital. I can't tell you how much that meant and still means to me. Thanks, in fact, to all of our friends, and very special thanks to Jen and Paul and Jill. Your friendship and support means the world to us, and we will always be grateful for it.

This book wouldn't exist without the many teachers and students at the University of Edinburgh who have shared their wisdom and friendship with me over the years. Special mention must go to Allyson Stack of the School of Literatures,

Languages & Cultures and to my comrade Beth Cochrane. Thanks to anyone who has ever considered themselves an Interrobanger, in any capacity at all. You know who you are. Thanks also to Ken Wilensky and Michael and Philip Vessa, and to Anushka Sinha, without whose wise counsel this book would have been completed under very different circumstances.

I very much appreciate the support of the magazines, newspapers and journals that have published my short fiction, narrative non-fiction and poetry, as well as the folks who have given me the opportunity to present various artistic endeavours in front of various audiences. Particular thanks are due in both of these regards to 404 Ink. Portions of this book originally appeared, in earlier and different versions, in 404 Ink Literary Magazine – Issue 3: POWER (December 2017) and in Marbles #3 (May 2018).

Building to a crescendo, special thanks to our families, who did what families are meant to do and came through and gave us their support when times were tough.

Finally, and most importantly, my eternal gratitude to Beth Monahan Brown, my muse, my patron and the love of my life. You started the process of saving my life long before the night of The Event, and you do it every day. It turned out that I did need you in my life, more than either of us could have imagined. Although somehow, I think I always knew.

This is, after all, a love story.

www.sandstonepress.com

 facebook.com/SandstonePress/

@SandstonePress